HEBREW SYNONYMS.

STUDIES

IN

HEBREW SYNONYMS.

BY
JAMES KENNEDY,
AUTHOR OF "AN INTRODUCTION TO BIBLICAL HEBREW."

PUBLISHERS
Eugene, Oregon

Wipf and Stock Publishers
199 W 8th Ave, Suite 3
Eugene, OR 97401

Studies in Hebrew Synonyms
By Kennedy, James
ISBN: 1-59752-668-1
Publication date 5/3/2006
Previously published by Williams and Norgate, 1898

TO

M. K.

PREFACE.

The publication of the following essays may be helpful in directing increased attention to a field of investigation which, although rather neglected, is nevertheless capable of yielding considerable fruit in return for careful cultivation. The material here presented will enable the reader to form a general estimate of the gains to Biblical science which may be derived from patient observation of the way in which even single words are employed by the writers of the Hebrew Scriptures.

In this department, more frequently than many imagine, it has been assumed that terms bearing the same general meaning, and presenting no perceptible difference in use, are really indistinguishable. This assumption has been further considered as confirmed by another, equally erroneous, regarding the parallelism prominent in Hebrew poetry. Here also it has been too commonly imagined that the different members present no practical difference of idea, the later members being substantially repetitions of the same thought as had been already expressed in the initial line. Indolence has here helped to confirm our ignorance. A sounder view of ancient Hebrew poetry, however, has conduced to the attainment of more accurate conceptions regarding the language generally. Happily, the conviction grows that there surely must be some distinctive difference in sense and use between different words in the same language. It is hardly reasonable to suppose that new words should be coined and put in circulation merely for variety, to bear exactly the same sense as other terms already used. We thus have warrant rather to assume that there must be some real difference in meaning when we find a difference of terms.

As the primary object in these investigations has been to determine the force and application, in Biblical Hebrew, of the words discussed, and to indicate as precisely as possible, in English, the ideas ordinarily associated with these terms in the minds of the Scripture writers, many interesting details have been intentionally omitted, as calculated to confuse the mind of the reader. Thus, it might interest many to compare the ascertained significations of the Hebrew terms with words of like import in other languages. Such connections, indeed, have occasionally been indicated, particularly when these analogous cases seemed likely to prove useful as illustrations; but as a rule they have been left unnoticed, lest they should distract attention from the main end in view. More especially, no endeavour has been made to point out the relation subsisting between the Hebrew words discussed and cognate terms in sister languages. Here, in particular, comparison may seriously mislead; for, even when the primary idea of the Shemitic root may seem to have been ascertained, the actual meaning of the term in Bible Hebrew may be metaphorical, and far removed from the original sense. Especially in the case of words rarely occurring in the Hebrew, but quite common in the cognate languages, where their use and meaning are indubitable, it is by no means safe to conclude that the Scriptural usage of the terms must be precisely the same as is proved for their congeners in the sister tongues. A fundamental likeness must indeed obtain throughout, but there is often an important difference, in sense or use, of the same term in different languages.[1]

Special caution is required with reference to later Hebrew. Even a slight acquaintance with Neo-Hebraic shows new shades of meaning still unknown in the Old Testament.[2] The influence of these later meanings on many Jewish writers is so strong, yet subtle, that some who have written on the present topic have been at times mis-

---

[1] A brief experience in learning French convinces us that 'je demande' is not exactly 'I demand,' that 'parents' are not what we understand by 'parents,' that when a French mother says 'mon enfant' she does not always mean her 'infant,' and that 'editeur' must not be always rendered 'editor.'

[2] Thus צְדָקָה 'righteousness' came to signify a kind of work-righteousness, viz. alms-giving (cf. the doubtful reading δικαιοσύνη or ἐλεημοσύνη in Matt. 6:1); לָשׁוֹן 'tongue' afterwards means a word, signification, etc. See a useful list of such words in Strack and Siegfried's Neuhebr. Sprache, S. 36. The transition to later usage is already visible in the Book of Ecclesiastes.

led, though all unconsciously, in their interpretations of the Scripture text. While many acute remarks and valuable hints are to be found in their writings, these must be read with caution and discrimination.

Two important advantages are derivable from such investigations. Firstly and directly, in determining the precise sense of words employed in Scripture, there is a distinct gain appreciable even by ordinary readers, but especially valuable and helpful to expositors. Secondly and secondarily, reliable guidance is afforded in recovering the true text of the Hebrew Scriptures,[1] which, through the failings of transcribers and from other natural causes, has in varying degree become corrupt, and hence at least obscure.

The literature on this subject is more extensive than might at first be supposed. So thorough and discriminating an account has already been given, by F. Mühlau, of works in this field, that we merely refer our readers to his remarks,[2] and add supplementary notes regarding treatises which have appeared since the publication of his paper. It unfortunately holds true that a merely historical interest attaches to most of the works he reviews, which were written without adequate consideration of the Scripture usage, many distinctions affirmed being purely fanciful or arbitrary. Of works mentioned by Mühlau, perhaps the most valuable are the few and rare dissertations by H. S. Reimarus,[3] the full and acute elucidations of S. Pappenheim,[4] unfortunately rather inaccessible; and the pleasant, pregnant hints of S. D. Luzzatto.[5]

Of treatises in Rabbinical Hebrew, published since Mühlau's article appeared, we may specify that of Abraham Bedarschi, whose valuable work remained in manuscript from the 13th century till a recent date;[6] of Moses Tedeschi, whose mechanical method of reducing the triliteral Hebrew terms to biliteral originals, in which he

---

[1] Examples of textual emendations thus obtained will be found on pages 13, 42, 69, 80, 99, and 129.

[2] Geschichte der hebräischen Synonymik, in the Zeitschrift der Deutschen Morgenländschen Gesellschaft, Band XVII (1863), 316-335.

[3] De differentiis vocum Hebraicarum, Wittebergae Saxonum, 1717-18, 4to.

[4] His work (in Rabbinical Hebrew) appeared at intervals, 1784-1831.

[5] These first appeared in his Rabbinical magazine entitled בִּכּוּרֵי הָעִתִּים, but have since been collected into a booklet, בית האוצר, Przemysl, 1888.

[6] The Hebrew title is ספר חותם תכנית, Amsterdam, 1865.

seeks the root-idea and by this fixes the sense, has diminished the value and importance of his work ;¹ and of M. Malbim, whose brief and methodical treatise,² though sometimes devoid of illustrations, shows careful observation and affords much help.

German scholars have produced a number of treatises, varying in compass and in value. C. Oswald, in a gymnasial programm,³ has given a succinct account of Hebrew verbs ; his remarks are generally just, and perhaps as fully illustrated as his limits would allow. C. von Orelli has discussed a single group of terms⁴ so thoroughly as to leave little that could be added to his remarks. With similar scholarship, but in more philosophic form, V. Ryssel has traced through the Shemitic languages generally another class of terms.⁵ The more extensive but far less intensive work of L. Kapff, posthumously edited by his friend L. Ableiter, is mainly a handy Hebrew vocabulary,⁶ with occasional remarks on synonyms. S. Levin has given us a small but welcome instalment⁷ of a systematic treatise ; while L. Kleimenhagen offers brief and unpretentious but sound remarks upon select groups of synonyms.⁸

In English, as yet, comparatively little has been published. The Hebrew Review for 1835-36 contains some short but helpful notes. Valuable hints may be gained from the laborious lexicon⁹ by Canon W. Wilson, of Winchester, though his remarks cannot always be justified. The brochures of E. G. King¹⁰ and A. W. Hands¹¹ are rather prefatory and inconclusive. But valuable results are given in the work of Canon R. B. Girdlestone,¹² despite undue deference shown to the Septuagint.

---

¹ Thesaurus synonymiiorum linguae Hebraicae. Padua, 1870.
² ספר יאיר אור, published at Warsaw, 1892.
³ Beiträge zur hebr. Synonymik, I. Theil : Verba. Stuttgart, 1869.
⁴ Die hebr. Synonyma der Zeit und Ewigkeit. Leipzig, 1871.
⁵ Die Synonyma des Wahren und Guten. Leipzig, 1872.
⁶ Hebr. Vocabularium in alfabetischer Ordnung. Leipzig, 1831.
⁷ Versuch einer hebr. Synonymik. Berlin, 1894.
⁸ Beiträge zur Synonymik der hebr. Sprache. Frankfurt a. M., 1896.
⁹ The Bible Student's Guide...2nd edition. London, 1870.
¹⁰ Hebrew words and synonyms : the names of God. Cambridge, 1884.
¹¹ Introduction to Hebrew synonyms expressing fear. Gloucester, 1891.
¹² Old Testament synonyms... 2nd edition. London, 1897.

CONTENTS.

1. Verbs signifying to flee ... ... page 1
2. Nouns signifying a wall 8
3. Verbs signifying to wash 15
4. Nouns signifying a lion 22
5. Words signifying sleep 26
6. Nouns signifying a fool, folly 29
7. Words signifying coal 40
8. Words signifying a flood 44
9. Words signifying oil 47
10. Adjectives signifying old 53
11. Words signifying weariness 63
12. Verbs signifying to hide, conceal ... 66
13. Adjectives signifying poor 81
14. Verbs signifying to pour out 92
15. Nouns signifying rain 105
16. Nouns signifying a rock, cliff, or crag ... 112
17. Nouns signifying a rod, stick, or staff ... 117
18. Nouns denoting ashes 131
19. Nouns denoting dust 136

HEBREW SYNONYMS.

1. Verbs signifying to flee.

a. נוּס,   *b.* בָּרַח,   *c.* נָדַד.

a. The specific meaning of נוּס is maintained throughout Scripture with remarkable uniformity : except in a very few passages,[1] this word is used with reference to *persons* seeking safety from danger in *open* flight, usually from a foe who sees and pursues. Naturally, the word frequently presents itself in records of warfare. A few of the many instances may be cited.

The first occurrence is in Genesis, chap. 14, which gives the account of the battle between the four kings and the five. We read that the kings of Sodom and Gomorrah, together with their allies, were defeated 'and fled (וַיָּנֻסוּ), and they fell there, while those who remained fled (נָסוּ) to the mountain' (v. 10). Again, on the destruction of Sodom, Lot entreatingly asked permission to enter the city of Zoar : 'Behold now, this city is near to flee (לָנוּס) thither......O let me escape thither,' Gen. 19:20.   Pharaoh

---

[1] Such are Isaiah 35 : 10 (repeated in 51 : 11), 'sorrow and sighing shall flee away;' Canticles 2 : 17, (also in 4 : 6), 'While the day is cool, and the shadows flee away, turn, my beloved;' Deut. 34:7, which says of Moses at his death that ' his eye had not dimmed, nor his freshness fled' (לֹא נָס לֵחֹה). The figurative language of Ps. 114 is obviously founded on the ordinary use of the word ; 'When Israel went out of Egypt,......the sea saw and fled (וַיָּנֹס), the Jordan turned back......What aileth thee, O sea, that thou fleest (תָּנוּס), thou Jordan, [that] thou turnest back ?'

and his host, after having pursued the Israelites into the bed of the Red Sea, became alarmed at their danger and exclaimed 'Let us [*lit.* me] flee (אָנוּסָה) from the face of Israel, because Jehovah fighteth for them ;' and when Moses had stretched out his hand over the waters, the sea returned, 'the Egyptians fleeing (נָסִים) against it,' Ex. 14 : 25, 27. After their first attack, the men of Israel were defeated and fled (וַיָּנֻסוּ) before the men of Ai (Josh. 7: 4); in the preparation for the second, Joshua, addressing those whom he placed in ambush, says of the inhabitants, 'when they come out against us, as at the first, then we shall flee (וְנַסְנוּ)) before them, and they will come out after us, until we have drawn them away from the city ; for they will say 'They are fleeing (נָסִים) before us, as at the first ; so we shall flee (וְנַסְנוּ) before them ; then ye shall rise up from the ambush, and take possession of the city,' Joshua 8 : 5—7 ; see also verses 15, 20. Sisera, defeated by Barak on the banks of the Kishon, 'fled (נָס) on his feet to the tent of Jael,' Judges 4 : 17, And in the last stage of the terrible struggle between the men of Benjamin and the other tribes of Israel, as recorded in Judges, chapter 20, we learn that while the latter at first made a strategic flight from their opponents (נָנוּסָה v. 32), the Benjamites in the end were utterly defeated and fled (וַיָּנֻסוּ) to the wilderness, finally taking refuge in the rock of Rimmon (verses 45, 47). The Benjamite who brought the fatal news regarding the capture of the Ark and the death of Eli's two sons, begins his story with the ominous words, 'I am he that came from the army, for I fled (נַסְתִּי) out of the army to-day ;' and when asked for further news, he proceeds, 'Israel is fled (נָס) before the Philistines,' 1 Sam. 4 : 16, 17 ; cf. v. 10.

These few specimens may suffice to show that נוּס properly indicates open and visible flight from danger; but reference may also be made to Josh. 10 : 11, 16 ; 1 Sam. 14 : 22 ; 17 : 24, 51 ; 31 : 1, 7 ; 2 Sam. 4 : 4 ; 10 : 13, 14, 18, (=1 Chr. 19 : 14, 15, 18) ; 18 : 3, 17 ; 24 : 13 ; 1 Kings 2 : 28, 29 ; 12 : 18 (=2 Chr. 10 : 18) ; 20 : 20, 30 ; 2 Kings 9 : 3, 10, 23, 27 ; likewise Lev. 26 : 17, 36 ; Deut. 28 : 7, 25 ; Prov. 28 : 1 ; Isaiah 10 : 29 ; 20 : 6 ; 24 : 18 ; 31 : 8 ; Jeremiah 46 : 5, 6, 21 ; 48 : 19, 44, 45 ; 50 : 28 ; 51 : 6 ; Amos 2 : 16 ; 9 : 1 ; Nahum 2 : 9 ; Zech. 14 : 5 ; Numbers 10 : 35 ; 16 : 34 ; Ps. 68 : 2. It should further be noted that this term is

VERBS SIGNIFYING FLIGHT. 3

invariably employed in all those passages where mention is made of the cities of refuge, to which the manslayer was to flee for safety from the avenger of blood : see Exod. 21 : 13 ; Num. 35 : 11, 15, 25, 32 ; Deut. 4 : 42 ; 19 : 3, 4, 5, 11 ; Josh. 20 : 4, 6, 9.

b. The proper and distinctive meaning of בָּרַח is that of *secret*, unobserved flight from danger, whether actual or expected ; to this use of the term, there is rigid adherence by the sacred writers. It is always applied to persons. From the very nature of the case, attempts to escape unobserved from the field of battle are impossible. It is thus obvious that this term can never be employed, like נוּס, in connection with open warfare, but we may well expect to find it used when mention is made of efforts by weak and timid natures to escape from danger, or even by those who, though not deficient in natural courage, are yet conscious of inferiority to a powerful foe, and deem it wise to run no risks.

The history of Jacob—as might have been expected—affords excellent illustrations. Thus, in Gen. 27 : 43, Rebekah counsels him in these words, ' Flee thou [secretly] (בְּרַח־לְךָ) to Haran, to Laban my brother.' Long after, on his return-journey from Haran, that time of weakness and secret flight from danger is recalled to the mind of the patriarch by God Himself, in the command, ' Arise, go to Bethel and dwell there ; and make there an altar unto the God that appeared unto thee when thou secretly fleddest (בְּבָרְחֲךָ) from the face of Esau thy brother, Gen. 35 : 1; see also v. 7, Hos .12:12. Jacob's timidity remains with him even after twenty years of sojourn in Haran : not courageous enough frankly to face Laban, he takes advantage of his father-in-law's temporary absence to steal away from Haran, ' for he told him not that he was fleeing secretly (כִּי בֹרֵחַ הוּא), so he secretly fled (וַיִּבְרַח), he and all that he had...... But it was told Laban on the third day that Jacob had secretly fled (בָּרַח),' Gen. 31: 20—22. And when the fugitives were overtaken, Laban gives unmistakable evidence, in his chiding, that the secrecy of the flight was what specially pained him: ' Wherefore didst thou flee secretly (לָמָּה נַחְבֵּאתָ¹ לִבְרֹחַ)?' v. 27.

---

¹ The idea of secrecy is brought into greater prominence by the verb here prefixed, with an adverbial sense, as in Isa. 55 : 7; Jer. 1 : 12; 49 : 8; 2 Kings 2 : 10, etc. (see also page 78).

But the term (בָּרַח) is also appropriately used when reference is made to the secret flight of stronger and more courageous souls. Even David often felt compelled to flee in secret from Saul, and prudently conceal his movements, as when his own house became unsafe, 'and he fled secretly (וַיִּבְרַח) and escaped, and came to Ramah, to Samuel, and told him all that Saul had done to him; and he and Samuel went and dwelt in Naioth,' 1 Sam. 19 : 18. But Saul pursued him even there, 'therefore he secretly fled (וַיִּבְרַח) from Naioth in Ramah, and came to Jonathan....' 20 : 1. Again, when the fugitive must remove himself from danger, David reaches Nob, where he receives, from Ahimelech, provisions and the sword of Goliath. Still is it unsafe to linger in that neighbourhood, 'so David arose and secretly fled (וַיִּבְרַח) that day for fear of Saul, and went to Achish, king of Gath,' 1 Sam. 21 : 10. As if to make amends for his disappointment at the escape of his son-in-law, the king of Israel vents his cruel rage upon the priests at Nob; but a specious excuse must be found for the unholy massacre; disloyalty is alleged, and complicity with David, as if they knew that he was fleeing in secret (כִּי־בֹרֵחַ הוּא) and did not inform the king, 1 Sam. 22: 17. A solitary individual—Abiathar, the son of Ahimelech—escaped 'and secretly fled (וַיִּבְרַח) after David,' v. 20. And a flood of light is thrown on the narrative of Absalom's rebellion, when we read that at a certain crisis the king felt constrained to say to his servants, 'Arise, and let us flee in secret (נִבְרָחָה), for [otherwise] there will be no escape from Absalom, 2 Sam. 15 : 14; see further 19 : 9; 1 Kings 2 : 7.

Other instances of prudent flight by men of undoubted courage may merely be mentioned. Even Jephthah deemed it expedient to effect secret escape from his hostile brethren, Judges 11: 3; Rezon, the powerful Syrian adversary of Israel, did not consider a secret flight from danger unbecoming, 1 Kings 11 : 23; and Jeroboam, knowing that his life was sought by Solomon, 'arose, and fled secretly into Egypt,' 1 Kings 11 : 40. And whatever opinion may be formed regarding their conduct as defenders of their country, it is enough for our present purpose to observe that king Zedekiah and his soldiers, on finding that a breach had at last been made in the walls of Jerusalem by the besieging force of Nebuchadnezzar, fled in secret (בָּרְחוּ) from the city through the night, Jer. 39 : 4;

VERBS SIGNIFYING FLIGHT.

52 : 7. For further illustration see Gen. 16 : 6, 8; Num. 24 : 11; Neh. 6 : 11; 13 : 10; Jonah 1 : 3, 10; Amos 7 : 12; Jer. 4 : 29; 26 : 21; Isa. 48 : 20; Ps. 139 : 7.

What has already been stated regarding the distinctive meanings of נוּס and בָּרַח will become still clearer when we now proceed to contrast the use of the terms in a few instances. Glancing at the history of Moses, we read that after slaying the Egyptian task-master, when Pharaoh sought his life, 'he fled,' Exod. 2 : 15; need it be said that the flight was in secret, and that therefore the term used in the original is בָּרַח? On the other hand, when we read that his rod, cast on the ground at the command of the Lord, had become a serpent, 'and Moses fled from before it,' Exod. 4 : 3, we feel prepared to find that the verb here employed is נוּס.

Turning next to the Book of Judges, we read, in chapter 9, of Jotham publicly addressing his parable to the men of Shechem, on the top of mount Gerizim, and then pointedly and boldly enforcing its meaning. That he should seek safety in immediate flight was but to be expected, and we read that 'he went to Beer and dwelt there, for fear of Abimelech, his brother,' v. 21. The precise force of the original Hebrew, however, at the beginning of the verse directly following the close of Jotham's address, is unfortunately lost in the 'Authorised' and the Revised versions, both of which render the words וַיָּנָס יוֹתָם וַיִּבְרַח 'and Jotham ran away and fled;' but a glance will at once show the inadequacy of this rendering.

Again, when Saul, sitting in his own house with spear in hand, attempted to transfix his son-in-law but missed his aim, through David's avoidance of the blow, the latter 'fled, and escaped that night,' 1 Sam. 19 : 10; the word employed to indicate this *open* flight, of course, is נוּס. But when, next day, the mad king sent to David's house for him, the fugitive betook himself to further *secret* flight by night; and, urged by Michal, who let him down through the window, 'he went, and fled, and escaped,' 1 Sam. 19 : 12; as might be expected, בָּרַח is employed to indicate this latter flight; see also v. 18.

Lastly, when Amnon had been openly assassinated by command of Absalom, fearing a similar fate, 'all the king's sons arose, and mounted each man upon his mule, and fled,' 2 Sam. 13 : 29 ; this flight, being *visible*, is properly designated by נוּס. But when we read, a little further on, that Absalom also fled, בָּרַח is the term employed, to indicate that his flight to Geshur was concealed, ver. 34 and 37.

c. It may have been already observed that both נוּס and בָּרַח have reference, more or less explicit, to a place of refuge as the termination of the flight. In this characteristic, both are distinguished from נָדַד, which primarily has a simpler sense, and means to flee from, shun, avoid, seek to escape from the presence of another ; this is seen in the complaint of the Psalmist, 'those who see me without flee from me,' (נָדְדוּ מִמֶּנִּי) Ps. 31 : 12 ; and in Nahum's prediction of Nineveh's desolation, 'every one who seeth thee shall flee from thee' (יִדּוֹד מִמֵּךְ) 3 : 7 ; also in the metaphorical application of the term to sleep, as in Esth. 6 : 1, 'On that night, the sleep of the king had fled ;' and Gen. 31 : 40, where Jacob, recounting to Laban his faithful and diligent service by night as well as by day, declares, 'sleep fled from my eyes.' Further illustrations are found in Ps. 68 : 12, ' Kings of armies flee, flee !' (יִדֹּדוּן יִדֹּדוּן) ; Jer. 4 : 25, 'I beheld, and lo, there was no man, and all the fowls of the heaven were fled' (נָדָדוּ) ; Hosea 7 : 13, where the Lord complains of Ephraim's apostasy, 'Woe unto them, for they have fled from me ;' see also Nahum 3 : 17, and Jer. 9 : 9.

Other elements usually included in the meaning of נָדַד are *dispersion* of the fugitives—if there be more than one—and *wandering*, without rest or refuge. These points are clearly presented in the following passages ; Is. 33 : 3, 'At the noise of the tumult the people have fled ; at the lifting up of thyself, the nations have scattered ;' in the woe pronounced by Jeremiah (49 : 5) against the Ammonites, 'Behold, I bring a fear on you, because of all that are round about thee, and ye shall be driven out, each one straight before him ; and there shall be none to gather the wandering fugitive' (מְנַדֵּד לַנֹּדֵד) ; in the words of Hosea denouncing Ephraim, 'My God shall reject them, because they hearkened not unto Him, and they shall be fugitive wanderers (נֹדְדִים) among the nations (9 : 17) ; and especially in the words of Isaiah's burden concerning Arabia (21 : 14, 15), 'To meet the thirsty, bring[1] water; O ye inhabitants of the land of Tema, go to meet the wandering fugitives (נֹדֵד) with their bread;' and in the description given by Eliphaz (Job 15 : 23) of the miserable state of the wicked, 'he fleeth about (נֹדֵד) for bread, [crying] Where is it?'

---

[1] In this passage, the imperatives seem preferable to indicatives.

2. Nouns signifying a wall.

a. חוֹמָה,   *b.* גְּדֶרֶת, גְּדֵרָה, גָּדֵר,   *c.* קִיר,
d. מַעֲקֶה,   *e.* חַיִץ,   *f.* שׁוּר.

a. The term חוֹמָה[1] is employed with the greatest uniformity to indicate a *town-wall*, or city wall,[2] strongly built for safety and defence,[3] and sufficiently thick to admit of one or more persons walking on the top (2 Kings 6 : 30 ; 3 : 27). An excellent illustration is presented in Joab's anticipation of David's outburst of displeasure on hearing that his men had suffered through too near an approach to the fortifications of Rabbah, 2 Sam. 11 : 20, 21 (cf. also ver. 24); 'Wherefore went ye so nigh unto the city? Knew ye not that they would shoot from the top of the wall (הַחוֹמָה)? Who smote Abimelek the son of Jerubbesheth? Did not a woman cast an upper mill-stone from the top of the wall, so that he died in Thebez? Why did ye go near to the wall?' Naturally also, frequent use is made of the word in the account of the restoration of Jerusalem, Neh. 3 : 33, 35, 38 [= 4 : 1, 3, 6, in English Bible], 'When Sanballat heard that we were building the city wall (הַחוֹמָה), he was angry ...and mocked the Jews... Now Tobijah the Ammonite was at his side, and said..., If a jackal go up, it will make a breach in their stone wall (חוֹמַת אַבְנֵיהֶם). So we built the wall, and all the wall was joined, as far as the half of it ;' see further 4 : 1, 4, 7, 9, 11, 13. In Ezekiel's prophecy against Tyre, chap. 26, there is frequent occa-

---

[1] Besides the plural חוֹמוֹת, there is used a peculiar dual form חֹמָתַיִם (double walls) Jer. 39 : 4 ; 52 : 7.

[2] τεῖχος as opposed to τοῖχος, or Lat. *mœnia, murus,* as distinguished from *paries, maceria.*

[3] In only a few passages is the word employed metaphorically ; thus Exodus 14 : 22, 29, 'The waters [of the Red Sea] were made unto them a wall on their right hand and on their left ;' 1 Sam. 25 : 16, 'They [David and his men] were a wall unto us both by night and by day.'

sion to introduce the word : 'Behold, I am against thee, O Tyre, and will cause many nations to come up against thee ; ...and they shall destroy the walls of Tyre (חוֹמוֹת צֹר)... Behold, I will bring upon Tyre Nebuchadnezzar king of Babylon...and he shall set his battering-rams against thy walls (בְּחֹמֹתָיִךְ) ; ...thy walls shall shake at the noise of horsemen and wheels, and chariots,...and they shall tear down thy walls, and break down thy pleasant houses' (vv. 4, 9, 10, 12). Reference may further be made to Josh. 6 : 5, 20 ; 1 Sam. 31 : 10, 12 ; 2 Sam. 20 : 15, 21 ; 2 Kings 3 : 27 ; 6 : 30 ; 18 : 26, 27 ; 2 Chr. 14 : 6 ; 32 : 5, 18 ; 33 : 14 ; Jer. 51 : 58.

b. גָּדֵר (const. גְּדֵר) together with the rarer cognate feminine form גְּדֵרָה,[1] and the still rarer גְּדֶרֶת, is never applied to any firm or solid structure, meant to be permanent, such as the walls of a house, but indicates a simply constructed wall of moderate height, formed of stones but without plaster, such as is frequently built to serve as the boundary-line of a field or some other kind of enclosure (Lat. *maceria*). An incident in the history of Balaam affords us a simple illustration. In Numbers 22 : 24, it is recorded that the place where the prophet was met by the angel of the Lord was a hollow way between the vineyards (מִשְׁעוֹל הַכְּרָמִים), a boundary-wall[2] being on either side (גָּדֵר מִזֶּה וְגָדֵר מִזֶּה). Again, in the touching parable of the vineyard, set forth in Isaiah (ch. 5), the Lord declares his purpose regarding faithless Jerusalem and Judah ; 'I will tell you what I will do to my vineyard,—remove its hedge, so that it will be consumed,—break down its boundary-wall (גְּדֵרוֹ),[2] so that it will be trodden down' (v. 5). Similarly, in the beautiful allegory of Ps. 80, the question is asked concerning the chosen vine, 'Why hast thou broken down her boundary-walls[2] (גְּדֵרֶיהָ), so that all those who pass along the way do pluck her?' (verse 13). See also Prov. 24 : 31.

Obviously, such a structure is comparatively slight, so that it may speedily be erected. Temporary or provisional walls of this character are then properly designated by גָּדֵר and its cognates, as in Ezekiel's outburst against the false prophets (13 : 5) 'Ye have not

---

[1] In Ps. 62 : 3, for the anomalous Masoretic reading גָּדֵר הַדְּחוּיָה, we must substitute גְּדֵרָה דְּחוּיָה.

[2] The rendering preferred in these passages by the Revisers is 'fence.'

gone up into the breaches and formed a wall (וַיִּגְדְּרוּ גָדֵר) for the house of Israel to stand in the battle in the day of the Lord;' and again, in Jehovah's bitter complaint (22 : 30), I sought from among them for a man who was building a [temporary] wall (גֹּדֵר גָּדֵר), and standing in the breach before me on behalf of the land, so that I should not destroy it, but I found none;' and yet once more, in the humble thanksgiving of Ezra (9 : 9), 'Our God hath not forsaken us in our bondage, but hath extended mercy to us in the sight of the kings of Persia...to set up the house of our God...and to give us a wall (גָדֵר) in Judah and in Jerusalem;' here it is significant that the pious and patriotic scribe does not employ the term חוֹמָה but uses a word that points to something far inferior. The slightness of such a structure is further shown by the application of the term גְּדֵרָה to a 'fold' for sheep, as in the pledge given to Moses by the Israelites who settled on the east side of the Jordan; 'Sheep-folds (גִּדְרֹת צֹאן) will we build for our cattle here, and cities for our little ones; but we ourselves will be ready, prepared [to go] before the Children of Israel until we have brought them to their place:' Num. 32 : 16; cf. vv. 24, 36; see also 1 Sam. 24 : 3; Zeph. 2 : 6.

c. That קִיר, as contrasted with גָדֵר and its cognates, nearly always indicates a compact structure—a firm and solid wall—becomes apparent on considering the passages in which the term occurs; it will also be seen that the word is very frequently used to denote a wall of any kind when viewed with special reference to its *side*. Let us illustrate these two points in order.

The mere fact that קִיר is the term employed when reference is made to the walls of a house—whether the outer walls or the inner partition-walls—might be deemed enough to show generally that such a structure is more substantial than what is indicated by גָדֵר. But this fact receives more distinct prominence in one of the symbolical predictions of the Exile delivered by Ezekiel (12 : 5, 7, 12), 'Prepare thee stuff for removing, and remove by day in their sight ...and thou shalt go forth thyself at even in their sight, as when men go forth into exile; dig thou through the wall (חֲתָר־לְךָ בַקִּיר) in their sight, and carry out thereby... And I did as I was commanded...and in the evening I digged through the wall with mine hand, and I brought it forth in the dark' (cf. ver. 12). Obviously,

NOUNS SIGNIFYING A WALL.

it is only through a solidly constructed wall that one could thus make an opening without bringing the whole to ruin. The very substantial nature of such a piece of work may be gathered from the mention of five cubits as the thickness of more than one wall (קִיר) in the Temple as seen and described by Ezekiel (41 : 9, 12).

But a more comprehensive illustration is presented in another of Ezekiel's prophecies recorded in chap. 8, where the prophet, after telling us that he was carried in spirit to the door-way of the court in the Temple at Jerusalem, proceeds to declare (v. 7-10), 'When I looked, behold a hole in the wall (חֹר אֶחָד בַּקִּיר). Then said he unto me, Son of man, dig now through the wall (חֲתָר־נָא בַקִּיר), and I digged through the wall, and behold, a door-way. And he said unto me, Go in, and see the wicked abominations which they are committing here. So I went in and saw, and behold, every form of creeping thing and abominable beasts, and all the idols of the house of Israel depicted on the wall (עַל־הַקִּיר) round about' (cf. 23 : 14). Remembrance of the fact, so patent in these closing words, that קִיר here signifies the *side* of the wall, will help to solve difficulties in other passages which will be cited hereafter. Further reference, however, may be made to other confirmatory instances, such as the first recorded attempt of Saul to take David's life, when the king, sitting in his house with spear in hand, while the youth played before him, cast the weapon, saying, 'I will smite David to the wall (בַּקִּיר) with the spear; but he slipped away out of the presence of Saul, who smote the spear into the wall' (בַּקִּיר) 1 Sam. 18 : 11; 19 : 10 (see also 20 : 25). We are reminded likewise of the circumstance that when Jezebel was thrown down from her window in Jezreel, some of her blood was spattered upon the wall (אֶל־הַקִּיר) and on the horses, 2 Kings 9 : 33; and that Hezekiah, on his sick bed, when warned by the prophet Isaiah to prepare for death, 'turned his face to the wall (אֶל־הַקִּיר) and prayed,' 2 Kings 20 : 2=Isa. 38: 2; see further Amos 5 : 19. Perhaps one of the plainest proofs, however, that the term applies to the side of a wall—outside and inside alike—is found in its metaphorical use to designate the sides of the altar (קִירוֹת הַמִּזְבֵּחַ) Exod. 30 : 3; 37 : 26; Lev. 1 : 15; 5 : 9; Ezek. 41 : 22. Noteworthy also is Isa. 59 : 10, where the prophet, describing the helpless condition of the people in the darkness of their sins, says, 'We grope for a wall (קִיר) like the blind.' Consider, further, the force of the expression מִשְׁתִּין בְּקִיר occurring in 1 Sam. 25 : 22, 34 ; 1 Kings 14 : 10, etc.

The foregoing results will sufficiently explain certain passages in which at first sight there might seem strange and unwarranted use of the terms. We have already seen that the place where Balaam's path was barred by the angel was in a low-lying road-way between the vineyards, a boundary wall (גָּדֵר) being on either side. But as the narrative proceeds, a change is made in the term applied to the structure: we read that 'the ass saw the angel of the Lord, and she crushed herself against the side of the wall (הַקִּיר) and crushed Balaam's foot against the side of the wall' (הַקִּיר) Numbers 22 : 25. The transition from one term to the other is obviously made with the utmost propriety and precision.

Again, in Num. 35 : 4, it is stated that the 'suburbs' of the Levitical cities were to extend a thousand cubits outward 'from the wall of the city.' Considering that there is a specific term appropriated to indicate a town-wall as such, one might have expected that the starting-point in this measurement would have been accurately enough expressed by חוֹמַת הָעִיר, but the terms actually employed are קִיר הָעִיר.

Most puzzling of all may at first appear the explanatory remark made in Joshua 2 : 15 regarding Rahab's assistance rendered to the spies ; 'she let them down by the cord through the window, for her house was on the side of the town-wall (בְּקִיר הַחוֹמָה),—since it was on the town-wall (בַּחוֹמָה) that she dwelt.'[1] But careful scrutiny of the terms employed only reveals the accuracy of the narrator's language.

d. The ἅπαξ λεγόμενον מַעֲקֶה signifies a *low wall or parapet* enclosing the flat roof of an Oriental house, and built as a safeguard. The legal injunction to the Israelite regarding this erection runs thus : 'Whenever thou buildest a new house, then thou shalt make a battlement (*or* parapet, מַעֲקֶה) to thy roof, that thou mayest not bring bloodshed upon thy house, if any one should fall therefrom,' Deut. 22 : 8.

---

[1] Even our Revisers have not given a quite satisfactory rendering of this verse, the latter part of which they translate thus: 'for her house was upon the town wall, for she dwelt upon the wall.'

NOUNS SIGNIFYING A WALL.

e. Another ἅπαξ λεγόμενον is חַיִץ, which seems from its derivation (חוּץ) to mean an outside wall. It is noteworthy that after the single mention made of the word, the more general term קִיר is substituted for it four times in the succeeding context. 'While one is building an outside wall[1] (חַיִץ) behold, they plaster it over with slime. Say thou unto those who are plastering it with slime that it shall fall; then shall be a sweeping rain (גֶּשֶׁם שׁוֹטֵף[2]), and ye, O great hailstones, shall fall, while a stormy wind shall rend it. And lo, when the wall (הַקִּיר) has fallen, will it not be said unto you, Where is the plaster wherewith ye plastered it?' Ezek. 13 : 10—12; see also verses 14, 15.

f. A third ἅπαξ λεγόμενον is כֹּתֶל, which occurs in Cant. 2 : 9, and judging from the kindred Arabic may probably mean a wall made of compacted clay, or like material closely pressed together. The context gives some support to the opinion that it may really be there applied to the walls of a house. 'My beloved is like a gazelle or a young hart: behold, he is standing behind our wall (כָּתְלֵנוּ) looking in at the windows, glancing through the lattices.' The opinion of some Rabbinical writers, that כֹּתֶל signifies a strong wall built of hewn stone, lacks confirmation.

g. The poetic term שׁוּר is found in only a few passages, where it plainly means something different from either חוֹמָה or קִיר, for it is neither a town wall nor the wall of a house, nor does it mean a low and slightly built wall or stone fence which one might overleap with ease, or overturn without much effort; it is rather a structure more than five feet high, so built that it might easily be scaled, but could not be destroyed without considerable difficulty. The passages in which this word occurs certainly induce us to think of a somewhat substantial wall, enclosing a garden or vineyard. And if the term be in any way connected with the verb שׁוּר 'to look,' we may further venture to think of the name as that of a wall erected in such a manner as not merely to enclose ground in which fruit is grown,

---

[1] The English marginal rendering, 'a slight wall' may possibly be an inference from the whole passage in which the word is found, but does not appear to be fully warranted.

[2] For the precise meaning of this term, see page 106.

but also to enable the watchers to mount on it with ease, and there gain a commanding view.[1]

The instances in which the term occurs are Gen. 49:22, 'Joseph is a fruitful bough,—a fruitful bough by a fountain; each of its branches mounts over the wall' (שׁוּר); 2 Sam. 22:30 [Ps. 18:30], 'By thee I rush a boundary-wall ([2] גְּדֵר), and by my God I leap a garden-wall' (שׁוּר); Job 24:11, 'Within their garden-walls (שׁוּרֹתָם) they press out oil; wine-presses they tread, and [yet] they suffer thirst.' The same meaning must be attached to the cognate שָׂרָה in Jer. 5:10, where the prophet momentarily refers to Jerusalem as the vineyard of the Lord, soon to be laid waste because of the iniquity of those within, 'Go ye up on her walls (שָׂרוֹתֶיהָ) and destroy, but make not a full end; take away her tendrils, for they are not the Lord's.'

---

[1] See foot-note on page 73.

[2] Klostermann's ingenious emendation (viz. גְּדֵר, instead of the Massoretic גְּדוּד) is obviously supported by the parallelism.

3. Verbs signifying to wash.

a. רָחַץ, *b.* הֵדִיחַ, *c.* כִּבֵּס, *d.* שָׁטַף.

a. Of all the Hebrew words which mean 'to wash,' רָחַץ is by far the most frequently used in Scripture. Its invariable application is to the bathing or washing of the *body*,—almost always the human body, rarely that of the lower animals. Here, as in so many other instances, the Hebrew suffers in comparison with the Greek, which, in its greater wealth of diction, has both λούειν (m. λούεσθαι) signifying 'to bathe,' *i. e.* to wash the whole body, and νίπτειν (m. νίπτεσθαι) to wash only in part;[1] the distinction is not made in the Hebrew, which has but the more general רָחַץ to cover both shades of meaning.

The widest application of this term, as the equivalent of λούειν and λούεσθαι, is exemplified in such passages as Ex. 29: 4, where the command is given to Moses regarding the initial rites of consecration to the priestly office; 'Aaron and his sons shalt thou bring near to the entrance of the Tent of Meeting, and thou shalt bathe (וְרָחַצְתָּ) them with water;' and again in the directions for the high priest in the solemn services of the Great Day of Atonement, 'he shall bathe (יִרְחַץ) his flesh in water, and put on the holy garments,' Lev. 16: 4; cf. also v. 24, and 22: 6. The same extended use (in a 'middle' sense) is presented in the command given by Elisha to Naaman, 'Go and bathe thyself (הָלוֹךְ וְרָחַצְתָּ) seven times in the Jordan,' 2 Kings 5: 10; in the words of Naomi to Ruth, 'Bathe thyself and anoint thee, and put thy garments upon thee,' Ruth 3: 3; and again, in the incidental remark concerning the daughter

---

[1] See the instructive passage, John 13: 10, ὁ λελουμένος οὐκ ἔχει χρείαν εἰ μὴ τοὺς πόδας νίψασθαι, and the remarks of Trench in his work on New Testament Synonyms.

of Pharaoh, Exod. 2 : 5, that she 'had come down to bathe by the Nile' (לִרְחֹץ עַל־הַיְאֹר).

The more restricted use of this term, as the equivalent of νίπτειν or νίπτεσθαι, is seen in the humble words of Abigail to David, 'Behold, thy hand-maid will be a maid-servant to wash the feet of the servants of my lord,' 1 Sam. 25 : 41 ; and in the several accounts of the hospitality displayed by Abraham to his heavenly visitants, Gen. 18 : 4 ; by Lot to the two angels, Gen. 19 : 2 ; and by Laban to the trusty servant of Abraham, Gen. 24 : 32,—water for washing the feet being provided on all of these occasions. The word is also employed when mention is made of Joseph washing his face, Gen. 43 : 31, and when Aaron and his sons received the standing ordinance to wash their hands and feet in the brazen laver before drawing near to minister at the altar, Ex. 30 : 19, 21 ; cf. 40 : 31 ; see also Deut. 21 : 6 ; Canticles 5 : 3. It is further worthy of remark that רָחַץ is the term usually employed in passages which describe the ritual of the burnt-offering ;[1] 'the inwards and the legs' of these sacrificial animals were always to be washed with water, obviously because such portions were peculiarly liable to defilement, Levit. 1 : 9, 13 ; 8 : 21 ; Ex. 29 : 17.

It is evident as well as important to observe that the washing indicated by רָחַץ, however full and thorough, can never effect more than *external* purification ; the inner substance or texture of what is subjected to this kind of cleansing remains quite unaffected and unchanged. The word thus points to *surface* washing at the most in any case.

b. The primary sense of הִדִּיחַ seems to be presented in Jer. 51 : 34 where the daughter of Jerusalem, bewailing Nebuchadnezzar's destruction of the holy city and the cruel treatment of its inhabitants who are driven into exile, exclaims 'he hath thrust me out' ([2] הֱדִיחָנִי). The point of the complaint is that she is cast out as an unclean thing,—thrust away as a defilement which may not be touched. Further examination seems to show that the normal use of this term is connected with the purging away of defilement, especially

---

[1] But see below.

[2] Throughout this passage, the Qeri gives the pronominal affix in the first person singular.

VERBS SIGNIFYING TO WASH.   17

from the carcases of animals which were being prepared as burnt-offerings, which symbolised perfect purity as well as complete consecration. In the description of the Temple seen in vision by the prophet Ezekiel, we read (40 : 38) that there was a chamber near the gates where 'they washed (יָדִיחוּ) the burnt-offering,' presumably from all kinds of impurity, but particularly clotted blood which still firmly adhered to the body of the animal. But as the water would need to be applied with some degree of force in order to remove the hardening matter, the expression 'purge' may perhaps best convey the idea of the original. Worthy of attention is the difference of terms employed in 2 Chron. 4 : 6, where, speaking of the ten brazen lavers made by Solomon for the Temple-service, the writer says, 'Whatever was prepared as a burnt-offering they used to purge (יָדִיחוּ) in them, while the sea was for the priests to wash themselves (לְרָחְצָה) in it.' And it is still with obvious allusion to the preparation of pure burnt-offerings that Isaiah thus prophesies (4 : 3, 4), 'he that is left in Zion and he that remaineth in Jerusalem shall be called holy, even every one that is written among the living in Jerusalem; when the Lord shall have washed away (רָחַץ) the filth of the daughters of Zion, and shall purge (יָדִיחַ) the blood of Jerusalem from the midst of her.'

c. The general meaning of the verb כָּבַס (πλύνειν) is fairly shown in its most common application to the washing of garments, an operation which, of course, can be properly performed only when the texture is cleansed throughout. The earliest occurrence of this term is in Exod. 19 : 14, where it is stated that 'Moses went down from the Mount [Sinai] unto the people, and sanctified the people, and they washed (וַיְכַבְּסוּ) their clothes.' This thorough cleansing of the garments is noteworthy as a symbolical act which was expressly prescribed in at least the more important cases of ceremonial purification, as a means of impressing on the minds of the Jews a deep sense of the all-pervading influence of unholiness. Whoever carried even a portion of the carcase of an unclean animal became himself unclean thereby, and was required to wash his clothes and remain apart until the evening, Lev. 11 : 25, 28; and whoever ate any part or carried the carcase of even a clean animal which had died of itself, had to undergo similar purification (v. 40); cf. 17 : 15.

B

Highly significant is the ordinance requiring that leprous clothing should be subjected to a double washing : 'the garment, either the warp or the woof or any article of skin, which thou shalt wash that the plague may depart from them,—it shall be washed (וְכֻבַּס) a second time that it may be clean,' Lev. 13 : 58. But this strict requirement is paralleled by that which demanded the double cleansing of every individual who had been freed from leprosy,—a second washing, not merely of his body but likewise of his clothes : 'he that is to be pronounced clean (הַמִּטַּהֵר) shall wash (וְכִבֶּס) his clothes, and shave off all his hair, and bathe (וְרָחַץ) himself in water, that he may be clean ; and afterwards he shall come into the camp, and shall dwell outside of his tent for seven days. But it shall be on the seventh day that he shall shave off all his hair,—his head and his beard and his eyebrows, even all his hair shall he shave off—and he shall wash his clothes and shall bathe his flesh in water that he may be clean,' Lev. 14 : 8, 9.

While the thoroughly defiling power of all unholiness, as that which completely permeates the whole nature of man, is thus emphatically set forth in connection with the law concerning leprosy, the divine requirement of entire purity, inward as well as outward, is likewise taught in other laws, though in a less striking manner. Leviticus, chap. 15, is wholly occupied with specifications of various kinds of bodily issues which caused defilement; but the ordinance regarding the removal of the uncleanness is always the same, viz. that the person defiled was to wash (כִּבֶּס) his clothes and bathe himself (רָחַץ) in water and remain unclean until the evening ; see verses 5, 6, 7, 10, 11, 13, 18, 21, 22, 27. It is further worthy of note that the person appointed to lead into the wilderness 'the goat for Azazel' on the Great Day of Atonement, as well as the man who burned the remains of the sin-offering outside the camp, could not be received again into the community of Israel till he had washed his clothes and bathed his flesh in water ; Lev. 16 : 26, 28. Similarly, both the priest officiating at the sacrifice of the red heifer, and his assistant who burned the ashes without the camp, thereby became defiled, and were required to wash[1] their clothes and bathe

---

[1] It is evident from 2 Sam. 19 : 25, Lev. 14 : 9, etc. that this verb כִּבֶּס occasionally bears the 'procurative' sense of getting another person to wash one's clothes.

VERBS SIGNIFYING TO WASH.

their flesh in water, remaining unclean until the evening, Numbers 19 : 8, 9 ; see also v. 10.

So far as we have yet seen, כִּבֵּס has been used solely with reference to the washing of garments. But what are we to say with regard to such passages as these,—Ps. 51 : 4, 'Wash me thoroughly (הֶרֶב[1] כַּבְּסֵנִי) from mine iniquity,' and v. 9, ' Wash me (תְּכַבְּסֵנִי) and I shall be whiter than snow ? ' Is this use of the term legitimate ?

It seems most likely that the Psalmist, keenly conscious of his deeply-rooted sinfulness, feels that no ordinary cleansing will avail to purify him from iniquity. His whole nature is defiled by sin, his every fibre foully stained; he knows he can be purified only by such a washing as will cleanse the inner man throughout. Hence, to use רָחַץ for expressing what he needs and seeks will not suffice, and might mislead ; to pray for outward purity alone is not enough. Then, even although the term might not be properly applied, yet, as the thought he would express is found in כִּבֵּס only, this he appropriates.

Similarly, in Jeremiah's warnings, this word obtains a fitting place, as when the prophet says, ' Wash (כַּבְּסִי) thine heart from evil, O Jerusalem, that thou mayest be saved,' 4 : 14 ; and again, when showing the utter futility of even the best endeavours of man after self-reformation, he says, ' Though thou wash (תְּכַבְּסִי) with lye, and take thee much soap, yet thine iniquity is written before me, saith the Lord God,' 2 : 22.

d. The proper meaning of שָׁטַף is indicated by the cognate noun שֶׁטֶף, which signifies an overpowering flood that sweeps along and carries off whatever cannot resist its force. The primary sense of the verb is exemplified in Is. 28 : 15, ' a sweeping scourge (שׁוֹט שׁוֹטֵף) when it passes along, shall not come unto us ; ' cf. also v. 18. When there is further assumed the secondary sense of washing, the original idea is not lost, but modified into the signification of *washing away by means of water in motion,* the impurity being carried off

---

[1] On the adverbial force of the first verb in this and similar constructions, see the author's Introduction to Biblical Hebrew, pages 174, 157, 163 ; Ewald's Hebrew Syntax, English translation, page 73 ; Gesenius' Hebrew Grammar, by Kautzsch, 26th edition, sec. 121, 2 *b* (sec. 142, 2 *b* in recent translations).

by the force of the current. The specific kind of washing signified by the verb שָׁטַף may thus most easily and naturally be effected in a running brook or streamlet; but the escape of water from a tap, or the pouring of water from a ewer, would equally fulfil the necessary conditions; even the dashing of water from a bucket or bowl fully satisfies all requirements. A few illustrations will suffice to make this plain.

Lev. 15:12 is rendered by the Revisers, 'And the earthen vessel which he that hath the issue toucheth, shall be broken; and every vessel of wood shall be rinsed in water' (יִשָּׁטֵף בַּמָּיִם). A similar example is found in Lev. 6:21 [v. 28 in English]: 'But the earthen vessel wherein it [viz. the flesh of the sin-offering] is sodden shall be broken; and if it be sodden in a brazen [copper] vessel, it shall be rinsed in water.' Further illustration is afforded by Lev. 15:11, a passage remarkable for the concurrence of synonyms demanding careful and accurate discrimination: 'And whomsoever he that hath the issue toucheth, without having rinsed his hands with water (וְיָדָיו לֹא שָׁטַף), he shall wash (יְכַבֵּס) his clothes, and bathe himself (וְרָחַץ) in water, and be unclean until the evening.' Obviously, however, the precise idea presented by the expression שָׁטַף בַּמָּיִם is somewhat different from that of 'rinsing in water,' so that this rendering rather misleads; but the English language does not possess the means of briefly and adequately representing the true sense of the Hebrew, as already explained.

Finally, the results now obtained enable us to read with fresh interest and more correct understanding the account of the last sad episode in the history of Ahab, 1 Kings 22:38. 'And they washed (וַיִּשְׁטֹף[1]) the chariot at the pool of Samaria, and the dogs licked up his blood, after the harlots had bathed themselves (וְהַזֹּנוֹת רָחָצוּ[2]), according to the word of Jehovah.' That the chariot was washed by means of water dashed against it is evident from the established meaning of the verb in the original. Further, the employment of רָחַץ which, we have seen, is exclusively used with reference to ablutions of the body, at once shows that the clause in which it occurs cannot be rendered (as in the Authorised Version and the margin

---

[1] This form is obviously the impersonal 3rd singular.

[2] This is a preteritive 'circumstantial clause;' see the author's *Introduction to Biblical Hebrew*, 2nd edition, page 235 f.

VERBS SIGNIFYING TO WASH. 21

of the Revised Version, following the Targum and the Syriac) 'they washed the armour;' nor again is it possible to entertain the suggestion of some that the harlots washed their clothes, or washed the chariot; but even the Alexandrian translators so far gave the sense correctly in their simple rendering καὶ αἱ πόρναι ἐλούσαντο. Read aright, how graphic is this word-sketch of a fitting end to an unhallowed life!

4. Nouns signifying Lion.

a. גּוּר, גּוֹר.   *b.* כְּפִיר.   *c.* אֲרִי, אַרְיֵה.   *d.* לָבִיא, לְבִיָא,

e. שַׁחַל,   *f.* לַיִשׁ.

Very definite conclusions may be drawn from Ezekiel 19 : 2, 3, 5, 6, where several different words are applied to the leonine family. 'What is thy mother? A lioness (לְבִיָא): between [full-grown] lions (אֲרָיוֹת) she lay down; amidst young lions (כְּפִירִים) she nourished her whelps (גּוּרֶיהָ). And she brought up one of her whelps; he became a young lion (כְּפִיר) and learned to tear prey, he devoured men... And she took another of her whelps; she made him a young lion. And he went up and down in the midst of full-grown lions; he became a young lion, and learned to tear prey, he devoured men.'

Another instructive passage is Nah. 2 : 12. 'Where is the den of the [grown] lions (אֲרָיוֹת), which is also the feeding-place for the young lions (כְּפִירִים),—where walked the [grown] lion (אַרְיֵה) [and] lioness (לָבִיא), [and] the cub of the lion (גּוּר אַרְיֵה), with none to make them afraid? The old lion (אַרְיֵה) tore enough for his whelps (גֹּרוֹתָיו), and strangled for his lionesses (לְבִאֹתָיו), and filled his caves with prey.'

a. גּוּר or גּוֹר (the forms being cognate) plainly signifies a *cub* or *whelp*, yet not merely and specifically the cub of a lion; for when employed in passages in which the context does not determine this to be the sense, and in which the application of the term is intended to be limited in this way, it becomes necessary to say גּוּר אַרְיֵה, as in Gen. 49 : 9, 'Judah is the whelp of a lion,' cf. Deut. 33 : 22; see also Jeremiah 51 : 38. In Lam. 4 : 3, the term is applied to the whelps of another wild animal.

NOUNS SIGNIFYING LION.

b. While כְּפִיר properly signifies a *young lion*, sufficiently large and strong to seek prey for itself (see Ezek. 19 : 2, 6, already quoted above, also Micah 5 : 7), it is manifestly impossible to say with precision when the term should cease to be applied to animals about a certain period of life, and one of the terms indicating a lion of mature age employed instead. It was evidently a lion at this transition stage which was killed by Samson, as recorded in Jud. 14 : 5 ff.; for, while the animal is at first designated כְּפִיר אֲרָיוֹת in v. 5, it is afterwards, in verses 8, 9, simply called אַרְיֵה, and אֲרִי in verse 18. Such pardonable vacillation regarding the exact word which should be used may have conversely led to the less warrantable employment of כְּפִיר for designating a lion in general, when אֲרִי or אַרְיֵה might rather have been expected; this usage, however, seems confined to the more strictly poetic parts of Scripture, as Jer. 25 : 38, 'He hath forsaken his covert, like the lion' (כַּכְּפִיר); Prov. 28 : 1, 'The righteous are bold as a lion' (כִּכְפִיר). In spite of such occasional interchange of terms, it is advisable to preserve the proper and specific rendering of each word as consistently as possible when both occur together, as in Job 4 : 11 ; Ps. 17 : 12.

c. By far the most common name applied to a *full-grown lion* is אֲרִי, or (much more frequently) אַרְיֵה;[1] it is also the most *general term* employed to designate the leonine family. The leading idea attached to these kindred forms is *surpassing strength*, but this is combined with a certain dignity. The אַרְיֵה is indeed terrible in its strength, yet does not simply delight in tearing; it has a native nobility. Maturity of bodily power and surpassing strength are implied in 2 Sam. 1 : 23, where David, lamenting the death of Saul and of Jonathan, exclaims, 'they were stronger than lions.' The same idea is specially prominent in the question, 'What is stronger than a lion?' Jud. 14 : 18; and it further seems noteworthy that, in Mic. 5 : 7, while the young lion (כְּפִיר) is represented as ravaging the flocks of sheep, the old lion (אַרְיֵה) attacks prey more worthy of his powers,—the large beasts of the forest (בְּהֲמוֹת יַעַר).

---

[1] That these words are interchangeable might be inferred from Judges xiv. where the longer form is used in verses 8, 9, while the shorter is employed in ver. 18; this is confirmed by a comparison of Gen. 49 : 9 with Num. 24 : 9; on the other hand, in 2 Sam. 23 : 20, where the Kethib is האריה, the Masoretes have expressly made הָאֲרִי the Qeri.

d. We have already seen that לָבִיא in Ezekiel 19 : 2 certainly signifies a *lioness*. The pointing of this form, however, is unique. Hitzig (commenting on Job 4 : 11) affirms that it should be altered to לָבִיא, which only occurs in about a dozen purely poetic passages, and this form, he thinks, must everywhere be regarded as signifying *lioness*. The opinion seems to be favoured by Job 4 : 11, which may well be rendered ' the young ones of the lioness (בְּנֵי לָבִיא) are scattered abroad ;' by Nahum 2 : 12 (given above) Gen. 49 : 9 (cf. also Numbers 24 : 9) 'he stooped down, he lay like a lion or like a lioness (כְּאַרְיֵה וּכְלָבִיא) : who will rouse him up ?' Job 38 : 39 'Wilt thou hunt prey for the lioness, or satisfy the appetites of the young lions ?' But the feminine meaning is not so urgently required in Num. 23 : 24 ; Deut. 33 : 20 ; Isaiah 5 : 29 ; 30 : 6 ; Hos. 13 : 8, so that לָבִיא might probably be a particular species of lion. The form לְבָאָה, however (Nah. 2 : 13), can only signify ' lioness.' On the other hand, the unique and poetic לְבָאִים (doubtless from לְבִי), in Psalm 57 : 5 bears the meaning ' lions.'

e. The word שַׁחַל is wholly poetic and comparatively rare. It is impossible to say whether a particular species of lion is designated,[1] or a lion of particular age. But all the passages in which it occurs plainly suggest fierceness or terror as the main idea with which the name is associated. We thus seem fully warranted in rendering the term, wherever it is found, by such an expression as a *fierce lion*. Psalm 91 : 13, ' Upon the fierce lion (שַׁחַל) and the viper shalt thou tread : thou shalt trample upon the young lion (כְּפִיר) and the dragon.' Prov. 26 : 13, ' The sluggard saith, There is a fierce lion (שַׁחַל) in the way, there is a big lion (אֲרִי) in the streets.' Job 4 : 10 ' The roar of the big lion (שַׁאֲגַת אַרְיֵה) and the voice of the fierce lion (קוֹל שַׁחַל) [are silenced], while the teeth of the young lions (כְּפִירִים) are broken.' This idea of terror as produced in the minds of men is likewise presented in Hos. 5 : 14 ; 13 : 7 ; Job 10 : 16, and 28 : 8.

f. Though לַיִשׁ occurs but thrice in the Scriptures, and there only in poetic passages, two of these throw very clear light on the term, which, if it does not designate the strongest and grandest

---

[1] Bochart held the opinion that it was the blackish lion of Syria.

NOUNS SIGNIFYING LION.

species of lion, must at least be a poetic name for a lion at its best, in the full maturity of strength, and with all the grandeur and dignity of its nature. In Proverbs 30 : 29, it is said that one of the 'three things which are stately in their march, yea, four which are stately in their going, is a lion (לַיִשׁ), which is mightiest among the beasts (גִּבּוֹר בַּבְּהֵמָה) and will not turn back before any one.' And in Job 4 : 11, it is said that the 'lion[1] (לַיִשׁ) perisheth from lack of prey,'—merely from hunger, want of food, but not through any decay of natural powers. Isaiah 30 : 6 sheds no further light on the meaning of the term.

---

[1] Certainly not ' old lion ' (A. V. and R. V.), if this expression be meant to indicate that the animal has passed its prime. Job 4 : 10, 11 is particularly rich in synonyms for ' lion.'

5. Words signifying Sleep.

a. { יָשֵׁן, שֵׁנָה. }   b. { נוּם, תְּנוּמָה, נוּמָה. }   c. { נִרְדָּם, תַּרְדֵּמָה. }

a. While the general idea of sleep is presented in the verb יָשֵׁן with its cognate noun שֵׁנָה and the participial adjective יָשֵׁן, these terms more frequently have special reference to that loss of consciousness which is at once natural and legitimate, the fit and proper restorative of bodily and mental powers which have been exhausted. Ps. 127 : 2 indeed, expressly says, ' It is vain for you who rise early, [and] who sit too late, who eat the bread of toil, [for] so he giveth his beloved sleep;'[1] while the Preacher also briefly and sententiously touches on the true relation of sleep to the circumstances of man when he declares (Eccl. 5 : 11), ' Sweet is the sleep of the labourer, whether he eat little or much ; but as for the abundance of the rich man, it will not allow him to sleep (לִישׁוֹן).' Further allusions to this divinely appointed sleep are found in Ps. 4 : 9, where the Psalmist says, ' In peace will I at once lie down and sleep (אֶשְׁכְּבָה וְאִישָׁן), for Thou, O Jehovah, alone dost make me to dwell securely ;' and again in Ps. 3 : 6, ' I' have lain down and slept (אֲנִי שָׁכַבְתִּי וָאִישָׁנָה), I have awaked, for Jehovah' upholds me.' Reference may likewise be made to such occurrences as Jacob's sleep at Bethel, during the first night of his journey to Padanaram (Gen. 28 : 16) ; to Pharaoh's sleep and dreams (Gen. 41 : 5) ; and to Elijah's sleep after his flight into the wilderness from the threatened vengeance of queen Jezebel (1 Kings 19 : 5) ; see also Jud. 16 : 14, 20 ; 1 Kings 3 : 20 ; Esther 6 : 1 ; Job 3 : 13 ; Prov. 4 : 16 ; Jer. 51 : 39 ; Ezek. 34 : 25. Few, comparatively, are the passages in which שֵׁנָה is associated with reproof, and these plainly point rather to abuse arising from excessive indulgence than proper use of a blessed gift : such is the warning in Prov. 20 : 13, ' Love not sleep, lest thou be reduced to poverty.' See, further, Ps. 13 : 5 ; Ps. 44 : 24.

---

[1] Or ' in sleep.' The singular form שְׁנָא is found only in this passage.

NOUNS SIGNIFYING SLEEP.

b. The idea of blameworthiness appears to be nearly always distinctly associated with the verb נום and its cognate nouns; indolent self-indulgence in sleep, at a time when one ought to be awake and active, seems essentially implied in all these words. This courting of sleep at improper seasons, and consequent neglect of duty, are well illustrated by the graphic description in Isa. 56 : 10, 'His watchmen are blind; none of them know; they are all dumb dogs [that] cannot bark,—dreaming, lying down [to sleep], loving to slumber (אֹהֲבֵי לָנוּם). This ceasing to watch, in order to enjoy the luxury of unconsciousness, with its dire consequences, is similarly sketched in bold outline by Nahum (3 : 18), 'Thy shepherds slumber (נָמוּ רֹעֶיךָ), O king of Assyria; thy mighty ones lie down to rest; thy people are scattered upon the mountains, and there is none to gather them.' The other side is shown in the description (Isaiah 5 : 27) of the keenly watchful and resolute enemies sent by Jehovah in his just anger against Israel; 'None shall be weary or stumble among them; none shall slumber or sleep (לֹא יָנוּם וְלֹא יִישָׁן) Still more striking is the touchingly simple and beautiful passage in Ps. 121 : 3, 4, 'Surely he will not (אַל) suffer thy foot to totter. Surely he that keepeth thee will not slumber (אַל־יָנוּם שֹׁמְרֶךָ). Behold, he that keepeth Israel shall neither slumber nor sleep (לֹא יָנוּם וְלֹא יִישָׁן).

The Book of Proverbs, as might have been expected, is not without its warnings regarding the consequences of slothful slumber; 'A drunkard or a prodigal shall come to poverty, and slumber (נוּמָה) will clothe [a man] with rags' (23 : 21); and again there is the pointed expostulation, 'How long, O sluggard, wilt thou lie down [to sleep]? When wilt thou arise from thy sleep (תָּקוּם מִשְּׁנָתֶךָ)? A little sleep (מְעַט שֵׁנוֹת), a little slumber (תְּנוּמוֹת), a little folding of hands for lying down [to sleep]; then shall thy poverty come like a robber, and thy want like an armed man' (6 : 9-11); see also 6 : 4; Psalm 132 : 4, and Job 33 : 15.

It may have been already perceived, from the illustrations now given, that in contrast with יָשֵׁן and its derivatives, which are used with reference to sound sleep, the verb נום is employed in speaking of lighter slumbers.[1]

---

[1] It is worthy of remark that in Arabic the case is reversed.

c. The noun תַּרְדֵּמָה signifies deep or heavy sleep, and the correlative verb נִרְדַּם (Niph.) means to fall into a deep sleep, to sleep heavily. The earliest occurrence of the noun is in Genesis 2 : 21, where we read that the 'Lord God caused a heavy sleep (תַּרְדֵּמָה) to fall upon the man, so that he slept (וַיִּישָׁן) ;' the second is in Gen. 15 : 12, where it is recorded that 'just when the sun was about to go down, a deep sleep fell upon Abram, and lo, an horror [of] great darkness fell upon him.' Illustrations of the verb-form are found in the history of Jonah, where we read (1 : 5, 6), in the account of the storm which arose, that the prophet 'had gone down to the sides of the ship and lain down and was sound asleep (וַיֵּרָדַם). And the master of the ship drew near to him and said to him, What meanest thou, heavy sleeper (נִרְדָּם) ?' The comparative ease with which Jael slew Sisera (Jud. 4 : 21) is not surprising, 'seeing that he was fast asleep (נִרְדָּם) ;' and sufficient explanation is given of the famous exploit of David and Abishai at the hill of Hachilah, when 'David took the spear and the cruse of water from Saul's head, and they departed, without any one seeing, or knowing, or awaking; for they were all sleeping (יְשֵׁנִים), because a deep sleep from Jehovah (תַּרְדֵּמַת יְהוָה) had fallen upon them ' (1 Samuel 26 : 12). Furthermore, we can readily perceive the point of the statement in Prov. 10 : 5, that ' he who sleeps heavily[1] (נִרְדָּם) in the harvest [is] a son that causeth shame.' Special attention is claimed by Psalm 76 : 6, 7, which contains a remarkable collection of synonyms ; ' The stout-hearted have let themselves be spoiled; they have slumbered into their sleep (נָמוּ שְׁנָתָם), and none of the men of might have found their hands. At thy rebuke, O God of Jacob, both horsemen and horses are fallen into deep sleep (נִרְדָּם).' See also Job 33 : 15 ; Isa. 29 : 10 ; Daniel 8 : 18.

---

[1] The rendering of the Authorised and the Revised Versions,—' he that sleepeth '—is inadequate.

6. Words signifying Fool, Folly.

a. כְּסִיל, כְּסִילוּת. *b.* אֱוִיל, אִוֶּלֶת. *c.* נָבָל, נְבָלָה.
d. סָכָל, סִכְלוּת.

a. Of all the words bearing the general meaning 'fool,' כְּסִיל is perhaps the most easily determined, inasmuch as most passages in which it occurs plainly indicate one who is foolish in *speech*—ignorant and thoughtless withal,—a person at once talkative and shallow, who shows greater readiness to utter whatever little is in his mind than to consider whether it might not be better to keep silence. Such folly, obviously, savours more of imprudence than of immorality, and in this respect widely differs from נְבָלָה: it is manifested by one who speaks more than he thinks, or who likes to speak rather than to think. Thus the כְּסִיל is a light-hearted, thoughtless, and noisy fellow, rather than a positively vicious person. It is only to be expected, therefore, that his folly should frequently be contrasted with ordinary prudence or wisdom, and this is actually the case in many passages of Scripture.[1]

The abstract noun כְּסִילוּת 'folly,' occurs only once, in Prov. 9 : 13, but its meaning there is perfectly patent, and amply confirms what has just been stated : 'A foolish woman (אֵשֶׁת כְּסִילוּת) is clamorous ; she is simple, and knoweth nothing.' The same combination of shallow ignorance and thoughtless talkativeness is plainly presented in many of the passages in which the concrete כְּסִיל is used, as Prov. 14 : 33, 'Wisdom resteth in the heart of him that hath understanding, but [that which is] in the inward part of fools is made known ;' 26: 6-9, 'He that sendeth a message by a fool (כְּסִיל) cutteth off [his own] feet, and drinketh in damage. The legs of the lame hang loose, so is a parable in the mouth of fools...As a thorn that goeth up into the hand of a drunkard, so is a parable in

---

[1] That the כְּסִיל is the opposite of the חָכָם will be evident from the illustrative passages which follow,

the mouth of a fool;' Prov. 18:6, 7, 'A fool's lips enter into contention, and his mouth calleth for strokes. A fool's mouth is his destruction, and his lips are the snare of his soul.'

The Book of Ecclesiastes also affords some excellent illustrations in which this form of folly is heartily condemned; thus 4:17 [Eng. 5:1], 'Keep thy foot when thou goest to the house of God, and be more ready to hear than to give the sacrifice of fools (פְּסִילִים);' the precise point of this exhortation is clearly shown in the succeeding verses, which continue in the same strain, 'Be not rash with thy mouth, and let not thine heart be hasty to utter anything before God; for God is in heaven, and thou upon the earth; therefore let thy words be few. A dream cometh with a multitude of business, and a fool's voice with the multitude of words. When thou vowest a vow to God, do not delay to perform it; for he hath no pleasure in fools (פְּסִילִים).' Eccl. 10:12, 'The lips of a fool will swallow up himself.' Further evidence that the פְּסִיל is a light-hearted and loquacious fool is found in Eccl. 7:4-6, 'The heart of the wise is in the house of mourning, but the heart of fools is in the house of mirth. It is better to hear the rebuke of the wise than for a man to hear the song of fools. For as the crackling of thorns under a pot, so is the laughter of the fool.' Additional proof that the פְּסִיל offends with his lips is afforded by such passages in the Book of Proverbs as 15:2, 'The tongue of the wise uttereth knowledge aright, but the mouth of fools poureth out folly;' 19:1, 'Better is the poor that walketh in his integrity, than he that is perverse in his lips and is a fool.'

The definite results now obtained enable us at once to determine the meaning of פְּסִיל in many other passages which otherwise would have been doubtful. It may be enough to cite merely a few of these, as Prov. 3:35, 'The wise shall inherit glory, but shame shall be the promotion of fools;' 10:1, 'A wise son gladdens a father, but a foolish son is the heaviness of his mother' (cf. also 15:20); 17:24, 'Wisdom is before the face of him that hath understanding, but the eyes of a fool are in the ends of the earth;' ver. 25, 'A son [who is] a fool is a grief to his father;' 18:2, 'A fool hath no delight in understanding;' 19:13, 'A son [who is] a fool is the calamity of his father, and the contentions of a wife are a continual dropping;' 23:9, 'Speak not in the hearing of a fool, for he will despise the wisdom of thy words;' 19 : 29, 'Judgments are prepared for scorners, and stripes for the back of fools;' 26 : 3, 'A whip for the horse, a bridle for the ass, and a rod for the back of fools;' 17 : 10, 'A rebuke entereth deeper into one that hath understanding than a hundred stripes into a fool.' But it is needless to cite further instances in which כְּסִיל is found: the Book of Proverbs abounds with them.

b. The precise signification of the term אֱוִיל is somewhat more difficult to ascertain, especially because this word, together with its cognate abstract אִוֶּלֶת 'folly,' is occasionally employed in a general manner. Yet it appears that there are at least two features specially prominent in this kind of fool,—first, a blind and stubborn self-conceit or self-sufficiency, based on ignorance or want of intellectual ability, so that אֱוִיל may be regarded as meaning a 'stupid fool;' and second, an impatience or irascibility of temper, which readily vents itself openly on the slightest provocation, especially when advice is offered, reproof administered, or any kind of opposition shown. Sometimes, but rather more rarely, a third element is brought out,—the wickedness of this folly.

The self-conceit of such fools is plainly indicated in passages like Prov. 1 : 7, 'The fear of the Lord is the beginning of wisdom, but wisdom and instruction fools (אֱוִילִים) despise;' 12 : 15, 'The way of a fool (אֱוִיל) is right in his own eyes, but he that is wise hearkeneth unto counsel;' 15 : 5, 'A fool despiseth his father's correction, but he that regardeth reproof getteth prudence;' 18 : 13, 'He who returneth answer before he heareth,—that is folly (אִוֶּלֶת) and shame unto him.' Further, the stubborn side of this foolish self-conceit is clearly presented in Prov. 22 : 15, 'Folly (אִוֶּלֶת) is bound up in the heart of a youth (נַעַר);' 27 : 22, 'Though thou shouldest bray the fool (אֱוִיל) in a mortar with the pestle among bruised corn, yet will not his foolishness (אִוַּלְתּוֹ) depart from him.'

Again, the unconcealed irritation of feeling, or annoyance of an אֱוִיל, arising from humbled pride after deserved rebuke, is apparent in Prov. 12 : 16, 'As for a fool, his vexation (כַּעְסוֹ) is openly known, but a prudent man concealeth shame;' 27 : 3, 'A stone is heavy, and the sand weighty, but a fool's vexation is heavier than them both;' and Eliphaz declares to Job (5 : 2), 'Vexation killeth a fool

(אֱוִיל) and jealousy slayeth the silly.' The general absence of self-control on the part of the אֱוִיל is further evident from Prov. 11 : 29, 'He that troubleth his own house shall inherit the wind, and the foolish shall be servant to the wise of heart;' while his proneness to make sudden and passionate displays of ill-temper is illustrated by Prov. 20 : 3, 'It is an honour for a man to keep aloof from strife, but every fool will be quarrelling;' 29 : 9, 'If a wise man have a controversy with a foolish man, whether he be angry or laugh, there will be no rest;' and the same passionate disposition is indicated in several passages where the cognate abstract noun אִוֶּלֶת 'folly' is employed, as Prov. 14 : 17, 'He that is short of temper committeth folly;' ver. 29, 'He that is hasty of spirit exalteth folly.' That the passion of the אֱוִיל may possibly sometimes even rise to fierceness is evident from Proverbs 17 : 12, 'Let a bear robbed of her whelps meet a man, rather than a fool in his folly;' and the overpowering influence of divine inspiration is sufficient to explain a statement which might otherwise have appeared unaccountably strange, 'The prophet is a fool (אֱוִיל), the man that hath the spirit is mad' (Hos. 9 : 7), the prophet, while in the ecstatic state, being so impassioned that he seems a raving fool or a madman.

That such a fool and his folly are even sometimes regarded as positively sinful is evident from a few passages in which אֱוִיל and אִוֶּלֶת occur, as Prov. 5 : 22, 23, 'His own iniquities shall overtake the wicked,...and in the greatness of his folly (אִוַּלְתּוֹ) shall he go astray;' 24 : 9, 'The thought of folly (אִוֶּלֶת) is sin;' Ps. 107 : 17, 'Fools (אֱוִילִים) because of their transgression and because of their iniquities are afflicted;' while the Psalmist (38 : 6) in deep distress acknowledges his iniquities, exclaims, 'My wounds stink and are corrupt because of my foolishness;' and in another psalm (69 : 6) there is even more distinct confession in the words, 'O God, *thou* knowest my foolishness, and my trespasses (אַשְׁמוֹתַי) are not hidden from thee.' In all these passages, the idea of guilt is undoubtedly attached to this kind of fool and his folly.[1]

But there yet remains a number of passages in which אֱוִיל and אִוֶּלֶת are evidently used to signify 'fool' and 'folly' respectively in a more general sense, so that it is difficult to determine in every

---

[1] Such applications of אֱוִיל and אִוֶּלֶת thus reveal an inclination towards the proper domain of the terms נָבָל and נְבָלָה, as will be explained below.

NOUNS SIGNIFYING FOOL, FOLLY.

case the precise meaning that may be intended ; indeed, there is an evident inclination to obliterate the distinction between כְּסִיל and אֱוִיל, especially through the almost complete disuse of the abstract noun כְּסִילוּת [1] and the employment, instead, of אִוֶּלֶת in conjunction with the concrete כְּסִיל. Illustrations of this tendency are found in Prov. 15 : 2, where it is said, 'The mouth of fools (כְּסִילִים) poureth out folly' (אִוֶּלֶת) ; ver. 14, 'The mouth of fools (כְּסִילִים) feedeth on folly' (אִוֶּלֶת); 12 : 23, 'The heart of fools (כְּסִילִים) proclaimeth folly' (אִוֶּלֶת) ; see also 13 : 16 ; 14 : 8 ; 26 : 4, 5, 11. Of the few passages in which אֱוִיל seems to be employed in a general sense, or even to be used instead of כְּסִיל, we may cite Proverbs 17 : 28, 'Even a fool when he holdeth his peace is counted wise ;' Job 5 : 3, 'I saw the foolish taking root, but suddenly I cursed his habitation ;' Jerem. 4 : 22, 'My people is foolish ; me they know not.' See also Prov. 10 : 8, 14, 21.

c. For determining the precise meaning of נָבָל 'fool,' 'foolish,' and of the cognate abstract noun נְבָלָה 'folly,' the most convenient course is to begin with the latter. Then it at once becomes evident that this word always signifies the folly of *wickedness*, and presents the idea of conscious, deliberate sin. It is further to be observed that the special form of impious folly to which the term is chiefly applied is any breach of the seventh commandment. Thus, it is said regarding the sons of Jacob (Gen. 34 : 7) that when they heard of the misconduct of Shechem towards their sister 'they were very wroth, because he had wrought folly (נְבָלָה) in Israel.' In the Book of Deuteronomy (22 : 21) it is appointed that proved infringement, by a woman, of the law regarding chastity, was to be punished with death, because she had 'wrought folly in Israel.' The same expression—perhaps a euphemism—is repeatedly employed whenever reference is made to the sin of the men of Gibeah, which entailed disastrous consequences on the whole tribe of Benjamin, as recorded in the latter part of the Book of Judges (19 : 23, 24 ; 20 : 6, 10) ; and Jeremiah, speaking for Jehovah against false prophets, declares (29 : 23), 'they have wrought folly in Israel, and have committed adultery with their neighbours' wives, and have falsely spoken in my name words which I commanded not.'

---

[1] See what has been already stated regarding this at page 29.

But though the expression עֲשׂוֹת נְבָלָה may be regarded as a frequent euphemism for denoting commission of sins of uncleanness, it is not wholly restricted to this use; for instance, it is applied to the sin of Achan in appropriating part of the spoils of Jericho; it is written regarding him that 'he transgressed the covenant of Jehovah and wrought folly in Israel' (Josh. 7 : 15). Isaiah in one of his prophecies against the kingdom of Israel (9 : 16, Eng., v. 17), speaking generally of their sinfulness as a nation, declares that 'every one is an apostate and an evildoer, and every mouth speaketh folly.' And finally, addressing Eliphaz, who with his two friends had been contending against Job, the Lord bids them offer sacrifices for their sins, and adds, 'my servant Job shall pray for you; for him will I accept, through his not committing folly with you' (Job 42 : 8). In all these instances, the 'folly' (נְבָלָה) to which reference is made is uniformly that of *sin*.

An easy and convenient transition from the consideration of the abstract נְבָלָה 'folly' to that of the concrete נָבָל 'fool' is presented in 2 Sam. 13 : 12, 13, where both words occur. Tamar, entreating Amnon to desist from his sinful designs, exclaims, 'Do not commit this folly,' and then she adds, 'thou shalt be as one of the fools in Israel.' But this is the only instance in which נָבָל is applied to one who offends against the commandment requiring chastity; in every other case, it is some other form of profanity or sin which is committed by the fool. Thus, it a blasphemous suggestion which Job condemns in his wife who urges him in his affliction and misery to 'curse God and die,' when he replies to her (2 : 10), 'Thou speakest as one of the foolish women (הַנְּבָלוֹת) speaketh.' Again, it is an impious desire and the practical rebellion of atheism that is condemned in Psalm 14 : 1 and 53 : 2, 'The fool hath said in his heart, There is no God.' It is dishonour to God which is denounced in Ps. 74 : 18, 'Remember this, [that] an enemy hath reproached Jehovah and a foolish people (עַם נָבָל) have blasphemed thy name,' and in v. 22, 'Remember thy reproach from a fool all the day.' Obviously also, it is an impious fool that we find in Is. 32 : 5, 6, 'A fool (נָבָל) will no longer be called noble (נָדִיב), nor a crafty one be named gentle. For a fool (נָבָל) will speak folly (נְבָלָה), and his heart will work iniquity' (אָוֶן). The sin of presumption is the particular form of impious folly condemned in Ezek. 13 : 3, where we read, 'Woe to the foolish prophets who walk after their own spirit and that which they have not seen;' while the reference in Jerem. 17 : 11 is to the sinful folly of injustice, 'He that getteth riches by unrighteousness —in the midst of his days he shall leave them, and in his latter end he shall be a fool;' and every one will readily perceive the point in Abigail's words to David concerning her husband (1 Samuel 25 : 25) 'Let not my lord, I pray thee, regard this man of Belial, Nabal (נָבָל), for, as his name is, so is he; Nabal is his name, and folly is with him.'

Since the term נָבָל has been clearly shown in the foregoing instances to signify an irreligious or godless fool, we may safely infer that it must bear the same meaning in other places where the context affords no clue to the specific sense. Among such passages are Psalm 39 : 9, 'Make me not the reproach of the fool;'[1] Deut. 32 : 6, 'Do ye requite this to Jehovah, O foolish and unwise people?' ver. 21, 'I will provoke them to anger by a foolish nation;' 2 Sam. 3 : 33 'Died Abner as a fool dieth?' Now also, by means of the results obtained, we are enabled to distinguish between one term and another, as in Prov. 17:21, 'He that begetteth a talkative fool (כְּסִיל) [doeth so] to his sorrow, and the father of an impious fool (נָבָל) hath no joy.' See also Prov. 17: 7; 30 : 21-23; Job 30 : 8.

d. The transition to סָכָל, סִכְלוּת and their cognate verb-forms סָכַל, הִסְכִּיל, נִסְכַּל brings us to another plane and another view-point than those of the terms we have just been considering. From a moral and distinctively religious ground we descend to a lower level on which advantage or profit is more regarded; from viewing conduct more or less in relation to the divine law, we come to consider human action rather in the light of its consequences or results, especially as these bring loss or damage to the doer. Sometimes, as we shall see, there certainly is a reference to divine commandment as the rule and standard of action; this class of terms, however, mainly regards the visible outcome or issue of actions as proved by their *results* to be unwise.

The use of the verb-forms most clearly reveals this feature. Thus Laban in chiding Jacob for his secret flight from Paddan-aram says (Gen. 31 : 28) 'Now hast thou acted foolishly' (הִסְכַּלְתָּ עֲשׂוֹ); and

---

[1] Cf. the more explicit utterances in Ps. 74 : 18, 22, quoted on page 34.

Saul, completely overcome by unexpectedly merciful treatment at the hands of David who had refrained from taking his life, exclaims (1 Sam. 26 : 21) 'Behold, I have acted foolishly (הִסְכַּ֫לְתִּי) and have erred exceedingly.' Samuel, reproving Saul for his self-will and presumption, declares (1 Sam. 13 : 13), 'Now hast thou shown thyself foolish (נִסְכָּ֫לְתָּ); thou hast not[1] kept the commandment of the Lord thy God which he commanded thee, for [if thou hadst obeyed] now would the Lord have established thy kingdom over[2] Israel for ever.' David, smitten with a sense of his sin after numbering the people (2 Sam. 24 : 10 ; 1 Chron. 21 : 8), exclaimed, 'I have shown myself very foolish (נִסְכַּ֫לְתִּי מְאֹד); and at a later period in Jewish history, when Hanani the seer is sent to reprove Asa for making alliance with Benhadad the king of Syria to help him against Baasha the king of Israel instead of relying on the Lord, the messenger declares (2 Chr. 16 : 9), 'Thou hast shown thyself foolish (נִסְכַּ֫לְתָּ) in this, for henceforth thou shalt certainly have wars.' But perhaps the clearest proof that this class of words mainly regards the final outcome or result of wrong or unwise conduct, as demonstrating its true character, is found in two passages where the Piël form of the verb is used in its factitive or declarative sense, viz. in 2 Sam. 15 : 31, where we read that David, seeking the frustration of what he knew must be cunningly devised plots against him, entreats the Lord, 'Stultify (סַכֶּל), I pray thee, the counsel of Ahithophel ;' and again, in Is. 44 : 25, where Jehovah is briefly described, in his overruling providence, as 'turning wise men backward, and proving their knowledge to be folly' (וְדַעְתָּם יְסַכֵּל). The best of human wisdom and forethought was thus to prove a miscalculation ; the most careful policy was to end in failure, as a blunder.

In proceeding further to consider סָכָל and its corresponding abstract סִכְלוּת, it seems worthy of special observation that, except in Jer. 4 : 22 and 5 : 21, these terms are used only in the book of Ecclesiastes, a work in which, among other matters, strong emphasis is laid on the need for prudence in the affairs of life. At intervals between the echoes of the opening sentence, ' Vanity of vanities,—

---

[1] If, instead of לֹא, we read לוֹ, the second part of the verse must be regarded as a purely hypothetical proposition (as in 1 Sam. 14 : 30 ; Job 6 : 2, 3) and more briefly rendered, 'if thou hadst kept..., surely now would...'

[2] Here we read עַל instead of אֶל ; the same correction must also be made in 2 Sam. 2 : 9 ; 6 : 3 ; 8 : 7 ; 20 : 23, and in many other instances.

all is vanity,' discretion and circumspectness are enforced as essential factors in safe and successful conduct. On the other hand, imprudence or miscalculation which results in failure is spoken of as blundering folly סִכְלוּת; while the unwise, indiscreet, or imprudent person who is incompetent to manage his own fortunes or those of others thereby proves himself to be a blundering and incapable fool סָכָל.

Let us begin with Eccl. 2 : 18, 19, 'I hated all the fruit of my toil for which I had toiled under the sun, because I am to leave it to the man who is to be after me. But who knows whether he will be a wise man or an incapable fool (סָכָל)? Yet he shall have full power over all the produce of my toil.' Let us next consider the advice given in Eccl. 7 : 16, 17, 'Be not very righteous, nor do thou show thyself exceeding wise (אַל־תִּתְחַכַּם יוֹתֵר); why shouldest thou make thyself forsaken [by others who will shun thee]? Be not very wicked, neither be thou an imprudent fool (סָכָל); why shouldest thou die when it is not thy proper time?' In both of these passages, סָכָל evidently means one who is deficient in practical sagacity, incapable of managing his own affairs with prudence and success. On turning next to Eccl. 10 : 5-7, we find reference made to incapacity for administering the affairs of others : 'There is an evil which I have seen under the heaven, as if it were an error which proceedeth from the ruler; an incompetent fool (הַסֶּכֶל[1]) is set in many a high position, while wealthy men sit in a low place. I have seen servants upon horses, while princes were walking like servants upon the earth.'

Having thus fairly ascertained the specific meaning of סָכָל in these passages, we may proceed with some confidence to assign the same signification to the term in other passages which might otherwise have remained doubtful, such as Jer. 5 : 21, 'Hear ye this now, O people blunderingly foolish (עַם סָכָל) and without understanding, who have eyes but cannot see, who have ears but cannot hear.' A distinct idea of the precise meaning, however, becomes all the more necessary in reading passages containing other terms of allied meaning; as Jer. 4 : 22, 'My people are blindly and stubbornly foolish (אֱוִיל); me they know not; blunderingly foolish (סְכָלִים) children

---

[1] We have ventured to change the vowel-pointing from the unique Masoretic form הַסֶּכֶל, the abstract meaning of which seems rather unsuitable here.

are they; wise are they to do evil, but how to do good they know not.' Special care must be taken to discriminate between the terms employed and at the same time to distinguish between the different persons indicated in Eccl. 10 : 2, 3, 'The mind of a wise man is at his right hand, whereas the mind of a talkative fool (כְּסִיל) is at his left. Moreover, on the way, when an incapable fool (סָכָל[1]) is walking along, he is wanting in his mind,[2] and says to every one [about the other], He is a blundering fool' (סָכָל הוּא). The illustrations already adduced may have sufficiently proved that כְּסִיל signifies one who is a fool in his *speech*, while סָכָל means a fool who shows himself to be such by his course of *action*.

It will be found that the attainment of the foregoing results is really necessary for acquiring definite ideas regarding the abstract noun סִכְלוּת, the precise meaning of which cannot be adequately determined solely through considering its context in any case ; now however, we may confidently regard it as denoting either the folly of *ineptitude*, or the blundering folly which, originating in the want of sufficient care and consideration, ends in disaster or ruin.

The several passages in which this term occurs are Eccles. 2 : 3, 'I searched in my mind how to cheer my flesh with wine—my mind guiding with wisdom—and to lay hold on ruinous folly (סִכְלוּת) till I might see what it is good for the sons of men that they should do under the sun.' Again, vers. 12, 13, 'I turned to see wisdom and madness and blundering folly (סִכְלוּת) ; for what [can] the man [do] who shall come after the king ?—just that which [others] did long ago. And I saw that there is a superiority to wisdom over stupid folly (סִכְלוּת) like the superiority of light over darkness.' Special attention is required in reading Ec. 7 : 25, 'I turned and my heart [with me] to know and to search out and to seek wisdom and consideration, and to know the wickedness of foolish talk (רֶשַׁע כֶּסֶל), —but thoughtless folly (הַסִּכְלוּת) is madness—and I find more bitter than death the woman who is [all] nets, and her heart deadly snares, her hands bonds ; [whoso is] good before God will escape from her, but a sinner shall be caught by her.' Eccl. 1 : 17, 'I gave my mind to know wisdom, and [get] a knowledge of madness and ruinous folly.'

---

[1] The Ke*tîb* הסכל, with the article in a generic sense, is quite defensible.

[2] לִבּוֹ חָסֵר (not 'his mind is wanting') ; usage elsewhere (Prov. 31 : 11 &c.) shows that חָסֵר refers directly to the *person* ; לִבּוֹ is thus a specifying accusative.

We are now in a much better position for dispelling some of the obscurity which overhangs other two passages in the Book of Ecclesiastes; the first of these is in 10:1, 'Every dead fly causes the ointment of a perfumer to give out a stench; [so] a little blundering folly (סִכְלוּת) outweighs wisdom and honour.' In other words, even a great and well-earned reputation for wisdom may be seriously affected by the unfortunate results of but one false step or miscalculation, a single act of indiscretion; and this observation of the Preacher reminds us of the maxim accepted and current among politicians and diplomatists of a certain school, 'A blunder is worse than a crime.'

The last passage is in the same chapter, verses 12-15, and here again the transitions from one to another of the terms signifying 'fool,' 'folly' must be carefully noted: 'The words of a wise man's mouth are gracious, but the lips of a talkative fool (כְּסִיל) swallow up himself; the beginning of the words of his mouth is blundering folly (סִכְלוּת) and the latter end of [the words of] his mouth is mischievous madness. But though the blundering fool (הַסָּכָל) may speak much, no man can know what is to happen; and as to what shall be after, who can tell him?'

7. Words signifying Coal.

a. גַּחֶלֶת. *b.* פֶּחָם.

Though coal is found in Lebanon, there is no evidence to prove that the mines were wrought in ancient times, and that the mineral was then used by the Hebrews. Hence, when 'coal' is mentioned in Scripture, the designation may with safety be understood as referring to another kind of fuel, viz. charcoal, rather than to the mineral with which we are so familiar: see especially Isa. 44:19; Ezek. 24:10 f. Ps. 120:4 is the only passage which refers to the specific substance of the coal, and there it is the wood of the broom (not 'juniper') that is mentioned.

a. There are but two words in Hebrew which may properly be rendered 'coal;' of these, the term which most frequently occurs is גַּחֶלֶת (plur. גֶּחָלִים). This has been regarded as always and only signifying a 'live' coal,—coal already kindled and burning, though in some cases perhaps merely smouldering. Such is certainly the meaning most generally associated with the word, yet it would seem that the acceptation of the term is not so restricted; for there are several noteworthy passages in which mention is made not simply of 'coals' but 'coals of fire' (אֵשׁ גַּחֲלֵי), as if the former of these terms, taken alone, might not be sufficient to convey the idea that the coals were lighted, burning. Thus, it was required of the high priest, among other observances on the Great Day of Atonement, that he should 'take a censer full of coals of fire from off the altar before the Lord, and his hands full of sweet incense beaten small, and bring it within the veil, and put the incense upon the fire before the Lord' (Lev. 16:12). Ezekiel in one of his visions (10:2) beheld a man clothed in linen who was commanded to go and fill his 'hands with coals of fire from between the cherubim, and scatter them over the city.' In another and still more remarkable passage in the prophecies of Ezekiel (1 : 13), the expression is even intensified by the superaddition of a strong participle : 'as for the likeness of the four living creatures, their appearance was like fiercely burning coals of fire (גַּחֲלֵי אֵשׁ בֹּעֲרוֹת), like the appearance of torches.' See further Ps. 18 : 13, 14 (cf. 2 Sam. 22 : 13), where the expression 'coals of fire' is twice employed. Would such intensive additions be made to the simple noun if the latter alone were always sufficient, with fulness and precision to convey the idea of a 'live' coal? The truth seems to be that גַּחֶלֶת is really a general term, and, when used alone, primarily indicates a black (i. e. unlighted) coal.

This is very plainly seen in Job 41 : 13, where it is said of leviathan that 'his breath kindleth coals (נַפְשׁוֹ גֶּחָלִים תְּלַהֵט) and a flame goeth forth from his mouth.' The point of this poetic description is that the breath of the monster actually kindles into flame and consumes[1] coals not previously lighted,—not merely fans into flame coals which have been already ignited.

It remains true, however, that this term, even if used by itself, may sometimes—at least inferentially—signify a lighted coal, as is evident from various passages. Prov. 6 : 28, 'Can a man walk upon the coals (הַגֶּחָלִים) and his feet not be burned?' Ezek. 24 : 11, 'Set it [viz. the caldron] empty upon the coals thereof (גֶּחָלֶיהָ), that it may become warm, and that the bronze thereof may be hot.' Consider also the classic passage in Isa. 44 : 19 exposing the utter folly of idolatry, 'I have burned part of it [viz. the tree] in the fire, yea also I have baked bread upon the coals thereof (גֶּחָלָיו);' Isa. 47 : 14 'There is no coal (אֵין־גַּחֶלֶת) to warm themselves at ;' Ps. 140 : 11 'Let coals fall upon them, let them be cast into the fire.' This meaning is further confirmed by passages in which the term is employed metaphorically, as in the address of the wise woman from Tekoa to king David (2 Samuel 14 : 7), 'They will quench my coal which is left ;' and the exhortation in Prov. 25 : 21, 22, well known through its citation by St Paul in Rom. 12 : 20, 'If thine enemy be hungry, give him bread to eat ; if he be thirsty, give him water to drink, for [thus shalt] thou be taking coals [and heaping them] on his head.' See also 2 Sam. 22 : 9 (Ps. 18 : 9).

---

[1] That this is the proper meaning of the verb will be apparent from other passages in which it is employed ; see Joel 1 : 19 ; Ps. 83 : 15 ; 97 : 3 etc.

b. The term פֶּחָם occurs but thrice in the Old Testament. The specific meaning commonly attributed to it is that of unignited coal, and some of the considerations which may have led to the formation of this opinion appear to have been that similar words in cognate languages, but notably the Arabic, point to some substance having a very black colour, coal; that this term might *a priori* be expected to show such a difference of meaning from גַּחֶלֶת; and especially that Prov. 26:21, where both terms are employed, seems to warrant the conclusion. But that פֶּחָם must rather signify only lighted coal —even blazing coal—is obvious from the other passages in which the word is used, viz. Is. 54:16, 'Behold, I have created the workman that bloweth a fire of coal' (אֵשׁ פֶּחָם), and 44:12, 'The smith hath sharpened [1] a chisel and worketh with the coal (הַפֶּחָם).' Does not the context in these passages compel us to think of the coal as *blazing?* Nor is this position at all untenable in Proverbs 26:21, '[As blazing] coal (פֶּחָם) to coals (גֶּחָלִים) [already burning], and [as] sticks to a fire, [so is] a contentious man to inflame strife;' indeed, to render פֶּחָם in this passage by 'fresh [i. e. unignited] coal' would be to miss the point of the whole sentence. It is thus evident that this word always indicates blazing fuel, and may in itself possess even a much stronger force than גַּחֶלֶת. It is further obvious from the instances cited, that פֶּחָם bears a collective sense, and hence should always be rendered 'coal' (not 'coals'); it never appears in the plural form.[2]

---

[1] In this obscure passage, it seems necessary to follow the Septuagint and to supply הִתַּד at the beginning of the verse, so as to correspond with ὤξυνεν.

[2] In Psalm 11:6, J. Olshausen reasonably reads פֶּחָם for פַּחִים, so that instead of the strange statement, 'Upon unrighteous ones he shall rain snares, fire and brimstone' (פַּחִים אֵשׁ וְגָפְרִית), we obtain a more probable description of the woe as 'coals of fire, and brimstone' (פֶּחָם אֵשׁ וְגָפְרִית).

Note.

Attention may here be directed to two cognate words רֶצֶף and רִצְפָּה which have often been erroneously rendered 'coal,' though really signifying something different. In 1 Kings 19:6, we read that on his flight into the wilderness lying to the south of Beer-sheba, there was provided for Elijah, in addition to a cruse of water, a cake baken on hot stones (עֻגַת רְצָפִים), for such—and not 'a cake baken on the coals,' though this opinion has the support of the Septuagint and of Rabbinical writers—is the correct meaning of the expression. This mode of baking cakes by laying them on flat stones which have been heated, is still habitual in the East. Again, in the account of the vision vouchsafed to Isaiah, when the awful majesty and holiness of Jehovah were revealed to him, we read that one of the seraphim took from off the altar 'a hot stone' (רִצְפָּה)—not 'a live coal'—with which he touched the prophet's lips (6:6). That this is the meaning of the term is proved by the fact that רִצְפָּה in all other passages where it occurs (Ezek. 40:17, 18; 42:3; Est. 1:6; 2 Chr. 7:3), as well as the kindred מַרְצֶפֶת (2 Kings 16:17), invariably means a 'pavement' formed of flat stones.

8. Nouns signifying a Flood.

a. מַבּוּל. *b.* שֶׁטֶף (שִׁטֶף), שֶׁצֶף.

a. The noun מַבּוּל is restricted in its application to the Flood in the days of Noah, generally called the Deluge. The Scripture record brings into prominence, as the distinguishing feature of that event, the outpouring of torrents of heavy rain (גֶּשֶׁם [1]) from above combined with the rise of the waters from beneath, causing the huge structure of the ark to float, and submerging even the lofty mountains, so that 'all flesh died that moved upon the earth' (see Gen. 7 : 11-21). The Noachian Deluge was thus not a torrent or a cataclysm which passed laterally over the surface of the earth, carrying off every object that lay in its course, but a mass of waters which rose from beneath and met with overpowering torrents that poured down from the heavens above, bringing destruction to every creature that lived and moved on the earth.

As the catastrophe is unique in the history of the world, so this term מַבּוּל is appropriated to denote that event; hence it is found only in those passages in the Book of Genesis which record the occurrence (Gen. 6 : 17; 7 : 6, 7, 10; 9 : 11, 15 etc.), and in the sole later allusion to the event in the words of Psalm 29 : 10, 'Jehovah sat [as King] at the Flood, yea Jehovah sitteth King for ever.'[2]

b. From what has been already stated,[3] we may be prepared to find that שֶׁטֶף (or שִׁטֶף) signifies a flood having a combined lateral and downward course,—that it denotes a mass of water sweeping

---

[1] See the remarks regarding this word in the chapter on 'Rain.'
[2] The Psalmist had already, in verse 3, pointed more generally to displays of the divine power within the same sphere: 'The voice of Jehovah is upon the waters; the God of glory thundereth; Jehovah is upon many waters.'
[3] See page 19.

WORDS SIGNIFYING A FLOOD.

along over a portion (merely) of the earth, overwhelming and bearing away, in its current, every removable object. All this is manifest even from the use of the cognate verb שָׁטַף in a number of passages such as Isa. 43 : 2, which contains the comforting promise, 'When thou passest through the waters, I will be with thee; and through the rivers,—they shall not sweep thee away' (וּבַנְּהָרוֹת לֹא יִשְׁטְפוּךָ[1]). Another (double) illustration is afforded in Jerem. 47 : 2, 'Behold, waters are rising up out of the north, and shall become a sweeping mountain-torrent (נַחַל שׁוֹטֵף[1]), so that they shall sweep (וְיִשְׁטְפוּ) the earth and what is therein;' and a third in the saddening complaint regarding the backsliders of Jerusalem, in Jerem. 8 : 6, 'Every one turned away in his rapid course, like a horse sweeping (כְּסוּס שׁוֹטֵף) through the battle.' See also Is. 8 : 8; 28 : 2; 30 : 28; Ps. 69 : 16; 78 : 20; 124 : 4; 2 Chr. 32 : 4 etc.

These passages give clear indication that by שָׁטַף we are to understand a *sweeping flood* or cataclysm, determinedly pursuing its way, seeking forcibly to carry off—perhaps to destruction—every object found in its course. It is thus specially appropriate for designating the swollen waters of the נַחַל or mountain-torrent in its headlong career, but it equally well applies to any more staid and slowly moving body of water,—provided always there is present the idea of overmastering power exercised in carrying off whatever cannot withstand the current. Very graphic is the description, in one of Daniel's visions (11 : 22), of the victorious career of a usurper and of the fate of his victims: 'With the arms of a sweeping flood shall they be swept away (וּזְרֹעוֹת הַשֶּׁטֶף יִשָּׁטְפוּ) from before him, and they shall be broken;' while another passage in a previous vision (9 : 26) with similar brevity depicts complete and overwhelming destruction: 'his end [shall be] with a sweeping flood' (קִצּוֹ בַשֶּׁטֶף). Like figurative language is introduced by Nahum (1 : 8) in setting forth the judgments of Jehovah on his enemies: 'With a sweeping flood passing away (בְּשֶׁטֶף עֹבֵר) shall he make a complete end;' and again in Prov. 27 : 4, 'Wrath is cruelty, and anger a sweeping flood; but who can stand before jealousy?' Finally, the idea that the course of even such a devastating body of water is after all confined within limits is distinctly presented in words of comfort for the godly (Ps. 32 : 6), 'Assuredly, as for a sweeping flood of many waters,—unto

---

[1] See the chapter on words meaning 'River, stream.'

him they shall not reach;' and again in the question addressed by the Lord to Job (38 : 25), 'Who hath cleft a channel (תְּעָלָה) for the sweeping flood?'

The term שֶׁצֶף occurs but once, in Isa. 54 : 8, and this under circumstances which suggest the conclusion that the prophet, for the sake of effect, has merely modified שֶׁטֶף so as to form a paronomasia thus : 'In a sweeping flood of wrath (בְּשֶׁצֶף קֶצֶף) I hid my face from thee for a moment, but with everlasting mercy have I had compassion on thee, saith thy Redeemer, Jehovah.'

9. Nouns signifying Oil.

a. יִצְהָר   *b.* שֶׁמֶן.

It must be borne in mind that the ancient Hebrews were quite ignorant regarding many different kinds of oil well known and much used outside the borders of Palestine. There is no evidence whatever to prove that they were acquainted with the preparation and employment of certain oils, derived from animal or vegetable substances well known to us and in common use among Gentile nations even in early times; while important mineral and other oils, discovered and utilised only in recent times, must of course be excluded from our thoughts in considering the passages, referring to oil, which are found in the Old Testament. It will be found, in fact, that the field of our investigations is very limited. Practically, we have but to consider *vegetable* oil, and this as derived from a single source, the *olive*.[1]

a. יִצְהָר is the proper designation for olive-oil at an early stage, i. e. oil viewed either as still contained in the berry on the parent tree, or as yet in the berry freshly gathered during the fruit-harvest, or at most but newly pressed from the fruit and not yet put to any specific use. In other words, יִצְהָר signifies olive-oil regarded merely as a natural product, directly contained in one of the fruits of the earth, but not yet adapted for use by man in any way.[2]

For, let it be carefully noted that the term occurs nearly always in the same connection, viz. as one element in the well known expression, 'corn and wine and oil' (דָּגָן וְתִירוֹשׁ וְיִצְהָר), or 'thy corn

---

[1] The expression שֶׁמֶן זַיִת 'oil of olive' (Exod. 27 : 20 ; 30 : 24 ; Lev. 24 : 2) may, however, be regarded as implicitly pointing, by contrast, to other sources.

[2] We are reminded of the distinction between δύναμις (*Lat.* potentia) and ἐνέργεια (actus).

and thy wine and thine oil,' a series of words which together indicate the entire grain-harvest with the vintage and the gathering of the olive-crop, but which scarcely point beyond, to the actual consumption of these fruits. For דָּגָן signifies but 'grain' in general, viewed as a product of the soil; it does not mean corn as prepared, ready for use as food. Further, תִּירוֹשׁ at most means 'new wine' (must), wine in its simplest and earliest form, as juice pressed from the grape; thus it differs from יַיִן in not yet having been subjected to those later processes in consequence of which it becomes 'wine' properly so called. In like manner, the third term in the triplet, יִצְהָר with which we are now concerned, is restricted in its application to the olive-oil at an early stage,—even still in the fruit, and this possibly not yet gathered from the parent tree; it signifies oil not yet fully prepared by man for his use, or actually applied to any particular object;[1] and there is always associated with the word some reference, more or less explicit, to the *harvest*. A few passages may be cited in illustration of these remarks.

Joel (1 : 10), describing the desolation of his country through the ravages of locusts and other devouring insects, exclaims, 'The field is wasted, the soil mourneth; for the corn (דָּגָן) is wasted, the new wine (תִּירוֹשׁ) is dried up, the new olive-oil (יִצְהָר) languisheth.' Haggai similarly unfolds the dealings of Jehovah in his displeasure with his negligent people (1 : 11) : 'I called for a drought upon the land and upon the mountains, and upon the corn and upon the new wine (הַתִּירוֹשׁ) and upon the new olive-oil (הַיִּצְהָר).' The actual harvest is much more frequently referred to, as in Deut. 11 : 14, 'I will give the rain of your land in its season..., that thou mayest gather thy corn and thy new wine and thy new oil,' and as in the similar words of comfort brought through Joel (2 : 19), 'Behold, I will send you the corn and the new wine and the new oil, and ye shall be satisfied therewith;' while a subsequent verse (24) in the same prophecy affords another illustration derived from a later stage in harvesting operations, 'The floors shall be filled with grain (בַּר), and the vats shall overflow with new wine and new oil.' In the many passages, also, which mention the presentation of first-fruits or the giving of

---

[1] The distinction between יִצְהָר and שֶׁמֶן finds a parallel in the relation of 'flax' (or lint), the natural product or raw material, to 'linen,' the prepared or manufactured article.

tithes, these same terms are properly employed; thus Deut. 18:4, 'The first-fruits of thy corn and of thy new wine and of thy new oil shalt thou give unto him' [viz. the priest; cf. also Num. 18:12]; or as in Deut. 12:17, 18, 'Thou mayest not eat within thy gates the tithe of thy corn, or of thy new wine, or of thy new olive-oil..., but thou shalt eat them before Jehovah thy God in the place which Jehovah thy God shall choose;' cf. 14:23, and see 2 Chr. 31:5; Neh. 10:38, 40; 13:5. Reference may further be made merely to the store-houses which were built by Hezekiah for holding 'the increase of corn, and new wine and new oil' (2 Chr. 32:28).

In these instances now cited, under the designation יִצְהָר the oil is obviously viewed in its origin,—still in association with its source in the olive-tree, or the berry within which it is immediately contained. It is thus, at this stage, regarded as a mere potentiality in relation to the wants or the convenience of man; for the term יִצְהָר by no means points to actual employment of the oil for any specific purpose, or even a state of readiness for use.

Regarding the interpretation of יִצְהָר in Zech. 4:14, see the conclusion of this chapter.

b. שֶׁמֶן, in contrast with יִצְהָר, is the proper term applied to olive oil when prepared and employed for a specific purpose, or at least when viewed in relation to actual use. Accordingly, שֶׁמֶן, and not יִצְהָר, is found whenever mention is made of oil as used for anointing, for lighting, for food,—in short, for any of the necessities or conveniences of human life, or for the service of Jehovah in the sanctuary.

A most striking and highly instructive passage is 1 Chron. 9:29, where mention is made of certain Levites who had charge, in the house of God, over 'the fine flour, the wine, and the [prepared] oil' (הַסֹּלֶת וְהַיַּיִן וְהַשֶּׁמֶן),—the terms are no longer וְהַתִּירוֹשׁ וְהַיִּצְהָר וְהַדָּגָן), for these materials were ready for being actually employed in the Temple service. Similar illustrative passages are Ezekiel 16:19, 'Fine flour, and [prepared] oil, and honey (סֹלֶת וְשֶׁמֶן וּדְבַשׁ) didst thou eat;' and v. 18, in which Jehovah, rebuking the idolatries of the inhabitants of Jerusalem, reminds them of the prepared oil and incense (שַׁמְנִי וּקְטָרְתִּי) with which he had provided them, but which they prostituted as offerings to idols; and only on the ground of

D

their being prospectively regarded as applied to actual use can we account for the singular mention, in Jer. 40 : 10, of wine and oil, in connection with the harvest, under the designation of יַיִן and שֶׁמֶן, rather than תִּירוֹשׁ and יִצְהָר: 'Gather ye wine, and summer fruit and oil, and put them in your vessels, and dwell in your cities which ye have seized.' Other like instances of such stores of provisions correctly designated, being ready for actual consumption, are found in 1 Chr. 27 : 28, 'Over the stores of oil (אֹצְרוֹת הַשֶּׁמֶן) [belonging to David] was Joash;' 2 Chr. 2 : 14, 'The wheat and the barley, the oil and the wine (הַיַּיִן וְהַשֶּׁמֶן) of which my lord the king [Solomon] hath spoken, let him send to thy servants ;' 11 : 11, 'He [viz. king Rehoboam] fortified the strongholds, and put captains in them, and stores of food, and oil and wine' (שֶׁמֶן וָיָיִן); see also Ezra 3 : 7 ; Jer. 41 : 8. General reference to the actual employment of oil for ordinary purposes is found in Prov. 21 : 17, 'He that loveth wine and oil shall not be rich,' in the account of Elijah's sojourn with the widow at Zarephath, during which the slender store of meal and oil was miraculously maintained (1 Kings 17 : 12, 14, 16) ; in the extraordinary increase, under Elisha, of another widow's oil, so that abundance was provided for redeeming herself and her sons from their heavy bondage of debt (2 Kings 4 : 1-7).

More specific reference to the actual employment of oil for a particular purpose is made in Deut. 28 : 40, 'Olive trees shalt thou have in all thy territory, but with oil thou shalt not anoint[1] thyself ;' in Mic. 6 : 15, 'Thou shalt tread an olive, but thou shalt not anoint thyself with oil ;' in Joab's command (2 Sam. 14 : 2) to the wise woman from Tekoah, 'Anoint not thyself with oil ;' in Ezekiel 16 : 9 ; Eccl. 9 : 8.

The term שֶׁמֶן is also applied (1 Sam. 10 : 1 ; 16 : 1, 13 ; 1 Kings 1 : 39) to the sacred oil for anointing ;[1] this unguent, however, on account of the peculiar mode of its preparation, and the spices with which it was mixed (Exod. 25 : 6 ; 30 : 23), frequently received a more specific name, as 'holy anointing oil' (שֶׁמֶן מִשְׁחַת־קֹדֶשׁ) Ex. 30 : 25, 31, 'the oil of anointing' (שֶׁמֶן הַמִּשְׁחָה) Exodus 25 : 6 ; 29 : 7 ; 31 : 11 ; 35 : 28 ; 37 : 29 ; 39 : 38 ; Lev. 8 : 30 ; Num. 4 : 16, 'the holy oil' (שֶׁמֶן הַקֹּדֶשׁ) Num. 35 : 25 ; Psalm 89 : 21, or 'the precious

---

[1] Regarding the difference between סוּךְ and מָשַׁח, see the chapter treating of verbs which signify to 'anoint.'

WORDS SIGNIFYING OIL.

oil' (הַשֶּׁמֶן הַטּוֹב), Is. 39:2; 2 Kings 20:13; Ps. 133:2. For giving light in the Holy Place, the lampstand (incorrectly called 'the candlestick') was supplied with 'the oil for the light' (שֶׁמֶן הַמָּאוֹר) Ex. 35:14; 39:37; Num. 4:16; it was required that this should always be the best, 'pure olive-oil, beaten' (שֶׁמֶן זַיִת זָךְ כָּתִית) Ex. 27:20; Lev. 24:2. In the service of the sanctuary, beaten oil was likewise mingled with the 'meal-offering' (מִנְחָה), Lev. 2:7; 7:10; 14:10; 23:13; Num. 28:5, 9. Unleavened cakes were mingled with oil, and unleavened wafers were anointed with oil, Ex. 29:2; Lev. 2:4; 7:12; Num. 6:15.

The results now ascertained enable us to set aside as unwarranted some interpretations of Zech. 4:14 which have been proposed by various expositors. This verse presents the concluding words in the account of a vision—confessedly difficult to understand in its entirety—in which the prophet beheld the seven-branched golden lampstand (מְנוֹרָה), with an olive-tree at each side. After receiving from the angel a message of comfort and encouragement for Zerubbabel in rebuilding the Temple,[1] the prophet enquires, 'What are these two olive-trees?...What are the two olive-branches which, by means of the two golden tubes, are those that empty the gold [coloured oil] out of themselves?...And he said, These are the two sons of oil (שְׁנֵי בְנֵי הַיִּצְהָר) that stand by the Lord of the whole earth.' In view of what has been shown regarding the distinctive meanings of יִצְהָר and שֶׁמֶן, it is plainly inadmissible to render שְׁנֵי בְנֵי הַיִּצְהָר by 'the two anointed ones,'[2] or by any similar expression in which explicit reference is made to *anointing*; if, however, in spite of the fact that the merely potential יִצְהָר (not שֶׁמֶן) is here employed, we are to regard a specific purpose for which the oil is ultimately used, then certainly the golden streams from the olive-tree compel us to think only of *illumination*. Strong as most expositors have felt the

---

[1] Some critics, however, excise the portion extending from 'This is the word of the Lord,' in ver. 6, to 'the hand of Zerubbabel,' in ver. 10, viewing this as a distinct prophecy, which they assign to a different time.

[2] Such is the rendering of the 'Authorised Version,' while the Revisers have contented themselves with the literal translation. The renderings given by one German commentator are 'die zwei Söhne des heiligen Oels,' and 'die beiden Gesalbten;' while another says, 'die Söhne des Oels sind die beiden Gesalbten, der König (in spe) und der Hohepriester.'

temptation to think concretely of Zerubbabel and Joshua, who were in those days the two most prominent personages among the Jews, each holding a sacred office, there is nevertheless, throughout this prophecy, no certain allusion to two anointed ones; there is at the most a general reference to two agents 'who stand by the Lord of the whole earth,' yet these may not be human beings after all; and though there is here inserted a special message for Zerubbabel, he cannot be regarded as anointed king. We thus rather seem called to think of the two 'olive-branches' as representing angelic mediators, appointed for the abundant ministration of divine grace which finally manifests itself in the form of 'light and leading.'

The assertion of Kliefoth, in commenting on this passage, that יִצְהָר signifies oil for burning in lamps, while שֶׁמֶן denotes oil for anointing, has already been proved groundless; but it is quite as erroneous to affirm against him that these terms 'are used promiscuously for either purpose, and both may have the same symbolic signification.'

10. Adjectives signifying Old.

a. יָשֵׁן. *b.* בָּלָה. *c.* זָקֵן. *d.* שָׂב.
e. יָשִׁישׁ. *f.* קַדְמֹנִי.

a. The term יָשֵׁן is never applied to persons or other living beings, to indicate advanced years, but only to inanimate things, i. e. it means 'old' as distinguished from 'fresh,' 'recent,' or 'new,' not as opposed to 'young.' Even within this restricted sphere, the lapse of a comparatively short time may suffice for allowing the proper application of this word, as is obvious from Cant. 7:14, 'At our doors are all kinds of precious fruits, both new and old (חֲדָשִׁים גַּם־יְשָׁנִים). Similar evidence is afforded in the provision promised by the Lord for the sustenance of man through the entire sabbatical year : 'I will command my blessing upon you in the sixth year, and it shall bring forth the produce for the three years. And ye shall sow the eighth year, and eat of the produce [what is] old' (יָשָׁן), Lev. 25 : 21, 22. Another illustration is presented in a later promise of the same kind (Lev. 26 : 10) : 'And ye shall eat old [provision] well seasoned (יָשָׁן נוֹשָׁן), and old in preference to new (יָשָׁן מִפְּנֵי חָדָשׁ) shall ye bring out.' Though it is obvious even from these instances that the advent of what is fresh or new (חָדָשׁ) necessarily causes what belonged to the preceding season to become relatively 'old' (יָשָׁן), this term does not by any means convey the idea that the thing to which it then properly applies has become useless,—unfit for further service.[1] This peculiarity in the meaning of יָשָׁן is further evident from other cases in which even many years may have elapsed before the appearance of the 'new' thing which required the attachment of the differentiating adjective 'old' to its correlative : instances of such a character are presented in Isa. 22 : 11, 'A reservoir ye made

---

[1] Contrast the meaning of בָּלָה, discussed on the following page.

between the two city-walls¹ (הַחֹמֹתַיִם) for the water of the old pool' (הַבְּרֵכָה הַיְשָׁנָה); Neh. 3 : 6, 'The old gate (²שַׁעַר הַיְשָׁנָה) did Jehoiada repair;' and in 12 : 38, where mention is again made of the same part of the city.

b. The adjective בָּלֶה, which but seldom occurs, signifies 'old' in the sense of being *worn out*, whether through the natural decay of fibre and strength in course of time, or through the tear and wear of use. In the latter case, the term might come to be employed after a comparatively brief lapse of time, and with reference to what in reality is not very old.

These observations point to the fact that this word is primarily and properly applied to material instruments which, owing to internal failure, no longer serve the purpose for which they were made. Thus we read (Josh. 9 : 4, 5) that the crafty Gibeonites, who imposed on the unsuspecting Israelites by representing themselves as having come from a distant land, supported the deception by bringing with them 'old [and worn out] sack-cloths (שַׂקִּים בָּלִים) for their asses, and old wine-skins (נֹאדוֹת יַיִן בָּלִים)..., and old shoes (נְעָלוֹת בָּלוֹת) ..., and old outer garments (שְׂלָמוֹת בָּלוֹת) upon them,' as well as dry and crumbled bread. But we also find the term applied, in Ezek. 23 : 43, to an old and worn out woman (בָּלָה), an adulteress.

These two are the only passages in which this adjective occurs; the meaning as now explained, however, is amply confirmed by others in which the cognate verb בָּלָה is employed: it may be enough to cite merely some of these. Passing over, with a simple allusion, the lying statement of the Gibeonites (Josh. 9 : 13) that the clothing and shoes they wore had grown old and become worn out (בָּלוּ) by reason of their very long journey, we find repeated reference to the miraculous preservation of the clothing worn by the Israelites during their long wilderness-life; in Deut. 8 : 4, Moses says to the people, 'Thy raiment hath not grown old (שִׂמְלָתְךָ לֹא בָלְתָה) neither hath thy foot swelled these forty years;' and again in 29 : 4, 'Your garments have not grown old upon you, nor hath thy shoe grown old upon thy foot;' see also the reminiscence in Neh. 9 : 21.

Simple but most effective allusion to such abolescence is some-

---

¹ See what has been already stated at page 8 regarding this word.
² Some prefer to render this 'the gate of the old [city-wall, *or* city].'

ADJECTIVES SIGNIFYING OLD.

times found in the poetic portions of Scripture; thus Isaiah (50:9) says, 'All of them shall wax old (יִבְלוּ) like a garment,' and again (51:6), 'the earth shall wax old like a garment;' while in Ps. 102 the contrast between the changeless Creator and the changeful creation is powerfully sketched in a few lines: 'they shall perish, but thou remainest, and they all shall wax old like a garment.' Noteworthy also are the words in Ps. 32:3, 'my bones waxed old (בָּלוּ) through my roaring all the day;' most instructive, however, on the point before us, is the question of the incredulous Sarah, on hearing the Lord's promise concerning her in advanced life (Gen. 18:12), 'After I am old [and worn out] (אַחֲרֵי בְלֹתִי), shall I actually have pleasure, my lord also being old [and growing feeble] (זָקֵן [1])? Her choice of the verb בָּלָה points to the fact that she had already reached that period of life when she could no longer hope to become the medium of bearing a son to Abraham,—that she was too old to become a mother.

c. The term זָקֵן is never applied to things, but only to *persons*. Even within this sphere, its use is more restricted than that of the corresponding English word might lead us to expect. For, in comparing the ages of two or more persons in early or even in middle life, the employment of זָקֵן was carefully avoided by the Hebrew; though we readily apply the terms 'old,' 'older,' together with their correlatives, to children as well as persons more advanced in years, the Hebrews used גָּדוֹל instead, in spite of the fact that the literal meaning of this word ('great,' or 'tall') points to size rather than age. Thus it is recorded that Solomon, after ascending the throne, says of his brother Adonijah (1 Kings 2:22), הוּא אָחִי הַגָּדוֹל מִמֶּנִּי, a statement which may be fitly rendered, 'he is my elder brother;' see also Gen. 10:21; 25:23; 1 Sam. 18:17; Ezek. 16:46.

Another fact to be observed is that נַעַר, which is commonly and sometimes very properly rendered a 'young man,' 'youth,' etc., is nevertheless by no means restricted in its application to one still in the early years of manhood. Joshua must have been older than what we usually understand by a 'young man' when he ministered

---

[1] Observe Sarah's introduction of זָקֵן to describe the condition of Abraham, after she has applied בָּלָה to herself; see also the concluding remarks on the former word at page 57.

in the tabernacle, though נַעַר is the epithet applied in Scripture (Ex. 33 : 11) to him at that period of his life. Absalom was not a mere stripling at the time of his rebellion, when his father David, in giving strict charge regarding the safe-keeping of his son, speaks of him as נַעַר (2 Sam. 18 : 5); and though Rehoboam is expressly declared to have been forty-one years of age when he succeeded his father Solomon (1 Kings 14 : 21 ; 2 Chron. 12 : 13), yet those who had been brought up with him, and who were therefore about his equals in age, are called נְעָרִים 'young men' (1 Kings 12 : 8, 10, 14); and his son Abijah, on referring afterwards to the revolt of the ten tribes, speaks of his father as being then—though aged forty-one— 'young (נַעַר) and tender-hearted' (2 Chr. 13 : 7).

Having thus seen that נַעַר is applied even to persons who have reached middle life, we are somewhat prepared for the conclusion that זָקֵן, together with its cognate nouns זִקְנָה and זְקֻנִים, as well as the verb זָקֵן, is used with strict reference to persons who really have passed their prime, and whose strength has already begun to wane. The ordinary correlative of זָקֵן is נַעַר; hence we find 'young and old' expressed in Gen. 19 : 4 and Josh. 6 : 21 by מִנַּעַר וְעַד־זָקֵן; in Isa. 3 : 5 we read 'the young man (הַנַּעַר) shall behave rudely to the old man'[1] (הַזָּקֵן); in Lam. 2 : 21, 'young man and old man lie upon the ground in the streets;' and in Ex. 10 : 9 occurs the bold declaration of Moses to Pharaoh, 'with our young men and our old men will we go;' see also Ps. 148 : 11; Jer. 51 : 22. Sometimes, however, instead of נַעַר we find בָּחוּר ('young man') associated with זָקֵן as its correlative; thus Jer. 31 : 13, 'young men (בַּחוּרִים) and old men together;' see also Lam. 5 : 14.

As the maturity of age mostly brings wisdom—the result of observation and experience during life—old men or 'elders' came to be appointed rulers over the community in which they lived. The honour and dignity of their position are well known, but it is worthy of remark that there were already 'elders' among the Israelites in Egypt before Moses and Aaron brought to them the message from Jehovah (Ex. 3 : 18; 4 : 29). Frequent mention is afterwards made of 'the elders of Israel' (Exod. 12 : 21 ; 17 : 6 ; 18 : 12 etc.), 'the elders of the congregation' (Lev. 4 : 15 ; Jud. 21 : 16), 'the elders of the people' (Ruth 4 : 4 ; Isa. 3 : 14). Obviously, it was of the

---

[1] Or 'elder;' the rendering 'ancient' is unwarranted and inappropriate.

ADJECTIVES SIGNIFYING OLD.

utmost importance, for the efficient discharge of their duties, that such זְקֵנִים should have as much as possible of the wisdom and gravity that ought to increase with years, but the minimum of weakness and decay that grow with age.

The weakness attendant on advanced life, however, may be assumed as an element nearly always implied whenever זָקֵן [1] or any of its cognate forms is employed; indeed, this idea is sometimes expressly indicated. Thus, in Gen. 48:10 it is said that 'the eyes of Israel were heavy by reason of old age' (מִזֹּקֶן); the Psalmist (in Ps. 71:9) utters the earnest prayer, 'Cast me not off at the time of old age' (לְעֵת זִקְנָה); in 1 Kings 11:4 we read that 'at the time of the old age of Solomon, his wives turned away his heart;' and later (15:23) that Asa in his old age was diseased in his feet; see also Gen. 18:11-13;[2] 24:36.

c. A further stage in human life is reached when we now come to consider 'hoary age,' or 'hoary hair' (שֵׂיבָה, but שָׂב in 1 Kings 14:4).[3] A brief but instructive illustration is presented in 1 Sam. 12:2, where the venerable prophet says of himself, 'I am old and hoary-haired' (וְשַׂבְתִּי), the second word in the description indicating advance beyond what is signified by the first term alone. The same distinction is presented in the comforting promise from the Lord to Israel by the mouth of Isaiah (46:4), 'Even to old age (זִקְנָה) I am he, and even to hoary age (שֵׂיבָה) I will carry you;' and again in the prayer of the Psalmist (71:18), 'Even to old age and hoary age (עַד־זִקְנָה וְשֵׂיבָה), O God, forsake me not.' This advent of life's winter with its snowy white, after the autumn maturity in man, is likewise touchingly presented in Prov. 16:31, 'Hoary age is a crown of beauty,' and once more in 20:29, 'Hoary age is the glory of old men.' In several passages also there is reference made to hoary age as the extreme limit of a desirable length of human life; to Abraham the promise was made (Gen. 15:15), 'thou shalt be buried in a good hoary age' (בְּשֵׂיבָה טוֹבָה), and the fulfilment is

---

[1] Compare the Latin *senex* and especially its cognate *senium*, which signifies infirm and burdensome old age.

[2] This important passage has been already quoted, in part, on page 55.

[3] The statement of some Rabbinical writers that זָקֵן denotes an old man up to the age of sixty, and שָׂב one between this limit and seventy, while יָשִׁישׁ applies to one who is still older, is rather rigid and wants confirmation.

recorded later (25 : 8), 'Abraham died in a good hoary age, old and full [of years].' Of Gideon also it is written (Jud. 8 : 32) that 'he died in a good hoary age;' while of David it is more fully stated (1 Chron. 29 : 28) that he died 'in a good hoary age, full of days.' See also Ps. 92 : 15 ; Gen. 42 : 38 ; 44 : 29, 31 ; Hosea 7 : 9 ; Lev. 19 : 32.

Finally, the far advance in age marked by the noun שֵׂיבָה is seen in what we read of its effects on the prophet Ahijah of Shiloh, regarding whom it is said (1 Kings 14 : 4) that 'his eyes stood [fixed and staring] because of his hoary age' (מִשֵּׂיבוֹ); and again, as we have already seen that נַעַר and זָקֵן are correlatives—forming, as it were, the two means in human life at its active stages—so the two extremes most commonly expressed are childhood proper and hoary old age, as illustrated in Deut. 32 : 25, where it is threatened that the sword shall destroy 'the suckling together with the man of hoary age' (יוֹנֵק עִם־אִישׁ שֵׂיבָה).

d. The very furthest advance in human life is marked by the adjective יָשִׁישׁ (once יָשֵׁשׁ), which can be applied only to a person in extreme old age; its simplest rendering is likewise the most appropriate,—'aged.' Of the few passages in which this word is found, perhaps the most instructive is Job 15 : 10, where Eliphaz, despising the arguments of the sufferer, but extolling the views advanced by himself and his friends, declares, 'with us are both hoary haired (שָׂב) and aged (יָשִׁישׁ), more in years than thy father.' Stronger contrast of terms is brought out at a later stage in some words uttered by the youngest of Job's friends, Elihu, who begins by saying (Job 32 : 6), 'I am young [lit. 'small in days' צָעִיר לְיָמִים], but ye are aged' (יְשִׁישִׁים); while another excellent illustration is found in 2 Chr. 36 : 17, where we read that Nebuchadnezzar, at the destruction of Jerusalem, 'had no compassion upon young man or maiden, old man or aged' (זָקֵן וְיָשִׁישׁ). See also Job 12 : 12, and 29 : 8.

e. The term קַדְמֹנִי signifies 'old' to the extent of being *ancient*, or belonging to the olden times; this reference to bygone ages distinguishes the word from זָקֵן, as well as from the other class of words just considered, which relate to the duration of human life. A simple illustration is afforded by the words of David to Saul, in

1 Samuel 24:13, 'As saith the proverb of the ancient [moralist] (מְשַׁל הַקַּדְמֹנִי), Out of wicked [men] cometh forth wickedness, but my hand shall not be upon thee.' Ezekiel, speaking in the name of the Lord (38:17), asks, 'Art thou he of whom I spake in bygone days (בְּיָמִים קַדְמוֹנִים) by my servants the prophets?' And Malachi, treating of the reformation to be wrought by the messenger of the Lord, declares, 'Then shall the offering of Judah and Jerusalem be pleasant unto the Lord, as in days of old and as in ancient years' (שָׁנִים קַדְמֹנִיּוֹת). See also Isa. 43:18.

11. Words signifying Weariness.

a. לָאָה, תְּלָאָה.   *b.* פָּנֵר   *c.* יָגֵעַ, יָגַע, יָגִיעַ.

d. יָעֵף, עָיֵף.

a. The weariness to which the verb לָאָה and its derivatives refer is not that naturally arising from bodily toil and exhaustion; it is rather the feeling of loathing or aversion in a discontented mind towards an unpleasant object, and thus has its seat in the soul or spirit rather than in the material frame. Exhausted patience, not exhausted physical strength, is implied; such weariness accordingly includes disappointment and vexation of spirit.

In the Book of Job (4:2), Eliphaz is represented as asking his afflicted friend, 'If one attempted to speak unto thee, wouldest thou be weary (תִּלְאֶה)?' And soon afterwards, in the same address, the speaker adds, 'Now it cometh unto thee, and thou art wearied' (וַתֵּלֶא), as if before the evil had actually been experienced. Very instructive also is the picture sketched in Prov. 26:15, 'A sluggard buries his hand in the dish; it wearies him to bring it again to his mouth;' the weariness certainly does not result from exhausted energy of any kind, but is merely the outcome of a discontented spirit. Such soul-weariness is again set before us in the complaints of the Lord against Israel: 'Your new moons and your appointed feasts my soul hateth (שָׂנְאָה); they have become a wearisome burden upon me; I am weariedwith bearing (נִלְאֵיתִי נְשֹׂא) them' (Is. 1:14); and again (Jer. 15:6), 'I am tired of repenting (נִלְאֵיתִי הִנָּחֵם).' Consider also the Lord's questions in Micah 6:3, 'O my people, what have I done unto thee, and in what have I wearied thee?' (הֶלְאֵתִיךָ) and in Is. 7:13, 'Is it a small thing for you to weary (הַלְאוֹת) men, that ye will weary (תַּלְאוּ) my God also?' See likewise Job 16:7; Jer. 6:11; 9:4; 20:9.

WORDS SIGNIFYING WEARINESS.

Having thus ascertained the proper sense of לָאָה and its derivatives in the passages now cited, we may confidently apply these results in fixing the meaning of certain passages which might otherwise be easily misinterpreted. In Gen. 19 : 11, we read that the Sodomites who had surrounded Lot's house were, for their wicked conduct, smitten with blindness, 'so that they wearied themselves (וַיִּלְאוּ) in finding the door.' But this weariness, we now perceive, was not so much of a physical as of a psychical character; the faintness was not caused by bodily fatigue but rather by loss of heart. Again, in Jer. 12 : 5, where the question is asked, 'When thou hast run with footmen and they have wearied thee (וַיַּלְאוּךָ), then how wilt thou rival the horses?' we perceive that the weariness was not so much that which results from exhausted bodily energy fruitlessly spent in the vain contest, as rather the weariness of discouragement arising from the consciousness of being defeated. Similarly, in Ex. 7 : 18, when Moses declared to Pharaoh that in consequence of the water in Egypt being turned into blood, the Egyptians would be 'wearied with drinking[1] (נִלְאוּ לִשְׁתּוֹת) water from the Nile,' we must understand the weariness as aversion to a hateful object, a weariness of soul.

The use of the cognate noun תְּלָאָה only serves to confirm what has now been stated. Part of Malachi's complaint against those to whom he addressed his message was that while outwardly professing to honour Jehovah, their heart was really far from him, so that they said of his service (1 : 13), 'Behold, what a weariness (מַתְּלָאָה) [it is]!' They were wearied, however, before they began. In Ex. 18 : 8, we read that 'Moses told his father-in-law all that Jehovah had done unto Pharaoh and the Egyptians on account of Israel, [and] all the weariness[2] (הַתְּלָאָה) that had come upon them in the way;' the word here employed to mark the experience of the wanderers points to the depressing influence of anxiety and care in face of difficulties, not to bodily exhaustion through the toil of travelling in the desert; see the similar use of the term in Numbers 20 : 14; Neh. 9 : 32; Lam. 3 : 5.

---

[1] Our English Version expresses the general sense very well in the rendering 'loathe to drink.'

[2] In the Revised Version 'travail,' or as in many editions of the Authorised Version, 'travel;' both forms convey a wrong meaning.

b. Though the general sense of the Piël-form פִּגֵּר might safely be inferred from the context in the single passage where it occurs, its precise and distinctive meaning is very clearly determined by the established sense of its cognate noun פֶּגֶר which is in frequent use, and always signifies a 'dead body,' corpse.[1] We are thus led to the conclusion that פִּגֵּר is a forcible term, meaning 'to be dead tired,' through complete exhaustion of bodily strength. This verb is, in fact, the strongest in meaning of all those which indicate weariness. It is only found in the account given (1 Samuel, chap. 30) regarding David's pursuit of the Amalekites, after they had seized and sacked Ziklag, and carried off the wives and children of David and his men. Of his six hundred followers, however, only two-thirds were sufficiently vigorous to overtake the enemy; for (ver. 10) 'two hundred stopped who were too thoroughly tired to cross over (פִּגְּרוּ מֵעֲבֹר [2]) the brook Besor.' See also the later reference (in ver. 21) to these two hundred who 'were too exhausted to follow (פִּגְּרוּ מִלֶּכֶת אַחֲרֵי) David.'

c. With the verb יָגַע is associated the idea of extreme weariness or fatigue that results from *exhausting toil;* the weakness, however, is of less degree than that which is marked by פָּגַר. Furthermore, it will be observed, from the passages in which this group of words is found, that the proper remedy for the kind of weariness to which they point is simply *rest;* a person described as יָגַע is too tired even to eat; and wherever this term or any of its cognates occurs, there is no mention of food or drink as a means for restoring exhausted strength. (Contrast the use of עָיֵף).

Highly significant, in one aspect, are Job's description of the state of the dead (3:17), 'There rest those who are exhausted in strength' (שָׁם יָנוּחוּ יְגִיעֵי כֹחַ); and the complaint in Lam. 5:5, 'We are wearied to exhaustion, and have no rest' (יָגַעְנוּ וְלֹא הוּנַח לָנוּ). Instructive also is the record (in 2 Sam. 23:10) regarding Eleazar, one of David's braves, that 'he smote the Philistines till his hand

---

[1] See Gen. 15:11; 1 Sam. 17:46; 2 Kings 19:35 (=Isa. 37:36); 2 Chr. 20:24, 25 etc. While this is the constant meaning in Hebrew, in Syriac, on the other hand, the word is sometimes applied to a living body.

[2] Contrast the force of the milder term עָיֵף, which is used in Judges 8:4, 5 (cited on the following page).

WORDS SIGNIFYING WEARINESS.

was completely wearied (יָעֲפָה יָדוֹ) and clave to the sword.' Moreover, we may now very clearly perceive the combined prudence and caution in the proposal made to Absalom by Ahithophel, to pursue David and capture him in the hour of extremity (2 Sam. 17 : 2); 'I shall come on him when he is utterly wearied' (אָבוֹא עָלָיו וְהוּא יָגֵעַ); effective resistance would then be practically impossible, and the fugitive king would become an easy prey. We are also in a position to understand the precise force of the Preacher's well known words (Ec. 12 : 12), 'Much study is an utter weariness of the flesh' (וִיגִעַת בָּשָׂר). Consider further Ps. 6 : 7 ; 69 : 4 ; Job 9 : 29 ; Josh. 7 : 3 ; etc.

At this stage, we are able to appreciate the distinction between different terms employed in Isa. 47 : 12, 13, where the Babylonian people are addressed as the daughter of the Chaldeans. 'Stand still now in thine incantations and in the multitude of thy sorceries in which thou hast utterly wearied thyself (יָגַעַתְּ) from thy youth. ...Thou art wearied (נִלְאֵית) in the multitude of thy counsels.' It is obvious that the former of the two verbs here indicated refers to exhaustion of bodily powers, the latter to mental weariness or distraction.

d. Regarding עוּף and its kindred יָעֵף [1] (which is not employed so frequently), it is to be observed,—

First, that the particular kind of weariness denoted, though corporeal, is not so great in degree as that to which יָגַע refers; the exhaustion is merely partial.

Second, that this kind of weariness is almost always induced by walking or running, and not by bodily exertion within a limited sphere of action.

Third, that the weariness is such as to admit of being readily alleviated or removed by partaking of refreshment, particularly drink ; reference to the latter is specially frequent.

These remarks receive ample illustration in various passages of Scripture. Gideon, following the fugitive Midianites, 'came to the Jordan, crossing over, he and the three hundred men that were with him, wearied (עֲיֵפִים), yet pursuing. And he said to the men

---

[1] The imperfect is always taken from the second of these two forms ; see Isa. 40 : 28-31 ; 44 : 12 ; Jer. 2 : 24 ; 51 : 58 ; Hab. 2 : 13.

of Succoth, Pray, give loaves of bread to the people that are following me, for they are weary (עֲיֵפִים הֵם), seeing that I am pursuing after Zebah and Zalmunnah, the kings of Midian' (Jud. 8 : 4, 5 ; see also ver. 15). In Gen. 25 : 29, 30, we read that when Jacob had been cooking pottage, his brother, doubtless after hunting, 'came from the field, weary (עָיֵף). And Esau said unto Jacob, Do let me devour some of the red, this red ; for I am weary' (עָיֵף אָנֹכִי). While these two cases distinctly exhibit solid food as the restorative for those who were faint or weary through partial exhaustion, a larger number of passages point to liquid nourishment employed for the refreshment of weary travellers. Thus, in Job 22 : 7, Eliphaz, accusing the afflicted patriarch, declares, 'Thou didst not give the weary (עָיֵף) [wayfarer] water, from the hungry one thou withheldest bread.' A familiar proverb runs thus, '[As] cold water to a weary soul (נֶפֶשׁ עֲיֵפָה), so is good news from a far country' (Prov. 25 : 25). More than one of the Psalms affords a touching illustration ; thus (63 : 2) 'My soul thirsteth for thee, my flesh pineth in a dry and weary (עָיֵף) land without water ;' and again (Ps. 143 : 6), 'My soul [thirsteth] for thee, as a weary land' (בְּאֶרֶץ עֲיֵפָה). Very clear proof is presented in Jerem. 31 : 25, where Jehovah promises restoration from captivity, saying, 'I have abundantly watered the weary soul (הִרְוֵיתִי נֶפֶשׁ עֲיֵפָה), and every soul [that] languisheth (נֶפֶשׁ הָאֵפָה) have I filled ;' also in 2 Sam. 16 : 2, where we read that the scheming Ziba, on coming to David with provisions, says, 'The bread and the summer fruit are for the young men to eat, and the wine is for any one who is weary (הַיָּעֵף) [through travelling and thirst] in the wilderness to drink.'

The definite testimony of these passages determines for us the meaning of עָיֵף in other instances, which, apart from such witness, might have remained at least doubtful. Isaiah (5 : 26, 27), predicting the advent of foreign foes, to execute the vengeance of Jehovah upon his apostate people, declares, 'Behold, they shall come quickly, swiftly ; none shall be weary (אֵין עָיֵף) and none shall stumble ;' again (28 : 12), 'This is the rest : give ye rest to the weary [one]' (לֶעָיֵף). Once more, the prophet (32 : 2), portraying good times to come, declares, 'A man shall be as a hiding-place from wind and a cover from a rain-storm [1] (זֶרֶם),...as the shade of a huge cliff [1] (סֶלַע)

---

[1] See the remarks on terms signifying 'rain' (p. 105) and 'rock' (p. 112).

in a weary land' (בְּאֶרֶץ עֲיֵפָה); and yet again, exposing the folly of the Babylonians in their idolatry, by showing that the national idols, Bel and Nebo, are a heavy burden rather than a help to their worshippers, he says (46 : 1), 'their images are [a burden] for the beasts and for the cattle ; your loads when lifted up [and] laid [upon the draught-animals are] a burden to the weary' [beasts=עֲיֵפָה]. In each of these instances, the weariness is that of the way-worn, whether man or beast; see moreover 2 Sam. 16 : 14 ; 17 : 29 ; Isa. 50 : 4 ; Jer. 2 : 24.

We are now in a better position for distinguishing between one and another of the words just considered. In Deut. 25 : 18, where the Israelites are commanded to remember and avenge the cowardly cruelty of Amalek, the reason is stated thus,— 'he met thee by the way and smote thee in the rear, all the weakest behind thee, whilst thou wast way-worn and exhausted' (וְאַתָּה עָיֵף וְיָגֵעַ). The closing word especially brings out the mean cowardice of the foe in attacking those who were not in a fit condition to offer effective resistance.

Finally, the results now obtained enable us to read, with fresh interest and more exact appreciation of its meaning, the well known passage in Isa. 40 : 28-31. 'Dost thou not know, or hast thou not heard [that] the eternal God, Jehovah, the Creator of the ends of the earth, neither becometh weary [with travel] nor is exhausted [with toil] (לֹא יִיעַף וְלֹא יִיגָע). There is no searching of his understanding. He giveth strength unto the way-wearied (לַיָּעֵף), and to those without power he giveth abundant vigour. Youths may grow weary [with travel] and become exhausted [with toil] (וְיָגֵעוּ יִעֲפוּ), and young men may utterly stumble (כָּשׁוֹל יִכָּשֵׁלוּ) ; but those who wait for Jehovah shall exchange strength [for yet greater strength] ; they shall ascend with wings like the eagles, they shall run and not be exhausted (יִיגָעוּ), they shall walk and not grow weary' (יִיעָפוּ).

See also Hab. 2 : 13 and Jer. 51 : 58 for other instructive illustrations.

12. Verbs signifying to hide, conceal.

a. טָמַן b. צָפַן c. הִסְתִּיר

d. עָלַם e. חָבָא, חָבָה

a. Some noteworthy features in the use of the verb טָמַן are revealed by the passages in which it occurs. (1) The word is almost exclusively applied to things,—material objects; in only a few instances is this term employed with reference to persons. (2) The hiding indicated is not relative, or partial, but absolute and complete; in this respect especially, the term differs from הִסְתִּיר. (3) The place of concealment is, normally, in or on the ground, about one's feet; at least, the place of hiding is below the ordinary level of human vision, so that one would have to look down in order to discover the object concealed. (4) The hiding, though intended to be wholly effective, is not deep; at best, the covering is slight and superficial.

In Gen. 35 : 4, we read that on the return journey to Bethel, Jacob's household gave him 'all the strange gods which were in their hand, and the ear-rings which were in their ears, and Jacob hid (וַיִּטְמֹן) them under the terebinth which was by Shechem;' in this as in other instances it is implied that the place of concealment was known only to him who hid the treasures; and Jacob intended that they should be buried without the possibility of discovery and recovery. Afterwards, we read that when Moses took the side of his fellow-Israelite against the oppressor (Exod. 2 : 12), 'he smote the Egyptian and hid him (וַיִּטְמְנֵהוּ) in the sand;' that Achan confessed the goods he had coveted and stolen from among the spoils of Jericho were 'hidden (טְמֻנִים) in the earth' in the midst of his tent (Josh. 7 : 21, 22); and later that the four lepers who were the first to discover that the Syrian host had fled (2 Kings 7 : 8), seized

VERBS SIGNIFYING TO HIDE, CONCEAL. 67

large spoil of 'silver and gold and raiment, and went and hid it' (וַיִּטְמְנֵ֥וּ[1]),—in the ground, of course.

The prophet Jeremiah (13 : 4-7) records that after the Lord had bidden him go and buy a new linen girdle, there came the further command, 'Take the girdle which thou hast bought, which is upon thy loins, and arise, go to the Euphrates and hide it (טָמְנֵ֖הוּ) there in the cleft of a crag (סֶ֫לַע[2]).' This divine command was obeyed, but after many days another was conveyed to the prophet: 'Arise, go to the Euphrates, and take from thence the girdle which I commanded thee to hide (לְטָמְנ֖וֹ) there. So I went to the Euphrates and digged (וָאֶחְפֹּ֕ר), and took the girdle from the place where I had hid it (טְמַנְתִּ֑יו).' On a later occasion, the same prophet (Jer. 43 : 9, 10) received a message to prophesy similarly by means of a symbolic act. 'Take in thine hand large stones, and hide them (וּטְמַנְתָּ֤ם) in the viscid clay in the brick-kiln which is at the entrance to the house of Pharaoh...Behold, I will send and take Nebuchadnezzar the king of Babylon, my servant, and I will set his throne above these stones which I have hidden' (טָמָ֑נְתִּי[3]). See also Job 3 : 16.

Significant and somewhat frequent mention is also made, particularly in the Psalms, of laying hidden snares and nets for entrapping the feet of the innocent and unwary. Thus Ps. 9 : 16, 'The nations are sunk in a pit they have made, in a net which they hid (טָמָ֑נוּ) is their own foot caught;' 31 : 5 'Bring me out of the net (רֶ֫שֶׁת) which they have hidden (טָ֣מְנוּ) for me;' 35 : 7, 8, 'Without cause have they hidden (טָֽמְנוּ) for me their net in a pit...Let destruction come upon him when he knoweth not; and as for his net which he hath hidden, let it catch himself;' 140 : 6, 'The proud have hid a snare (פַּח) for me, and cords; they have spread a net by the side of the way;' 142 : 4, 'In the way wherein I walk have they hid a snare (טָֽמְנוּ־פַ֑ח) for me;' Jer. 18 : 22, 'Snares have they hidden (פַּחִ֖ים טָ֣מְנוּ) for my

---

[1] This Hiphil form is unique, but the pointing may safely be changed to that of Qal (וַיִּטְמְנוּ), inasmuch as no difference of meaning is involved.

[2] See the subsequent remarks on words signifying 'rock,' 'crag.'

[3] A more probable reading here is טָמַ֫נְתָּ ('thou [Jeremiah] hast hidden'); this is supported not only by the Septuagint κατέκρυψας but also by the preceding context. Similarly, in Ps. 31 : 7, instead of שָׂנֵ֫אתִי ('I hate'), the Septuagint ἐμίσησας points to שָׂנֵ֫אתָ; and further, in 89 : 3, for אָמַ֫רְתִּי it may be better to read אָמַ֫רְתָּ, the Greek version having εἶπας.

feet;' Job 18 : 10, 'His cord [snare] is hid (טָמוּן) in the earth, and his trap on a foot-path.' See also Ps. 64 : 6.

These passages amply illustrate the normal sense and application of this verb; deviations are but few. In some rare instances the term, although applied to persons, yet retains the sense of hiding in the ground, or at least near the ordinary level for walking. Isaiah (2 : 10), after briefly describing the apostasy and idolatry of Israel, directly addresses the guilty, in view of the approaching day of the Lord : 'Enter into the rock, and hide thyself (הִטָּמֵן) in the dust.' Reproving Job (40 : 12, 13), the Lord commands, 'Look on every proud one, make him bow down, and tread down the unrighteous ones on the spot (תַּחְתָּם). Hide them (טָמְנֵם) in the dust together; bind their persons in the hidden place' (בַּטָּמוּן) [under the soil]. And in Josh. 2 : 6 we read that Rahab, to save the Hebrew spies that had come into her house, 'brought them up to the roof and hid them (וַתִּטְמְנֵם) with the flax which had been laid in order by her upon the roof.'

In a very few remaining instances, the place of concealment, though not on the ground, is nevertheless below the common level of human vision; and the hiding, though complete, is not deep. Thus Prov. 19 : 24, 'A sluggard burieth (טָמַן) his hand in the dish; he will not return it even to his mouth,' and the parallel in 26 : 15, 'A sluggard burieth his hand in the dish; he feels wearied (נִלְאָה[1]) to return it to his mouth.'

This idea of complete concealment beneath a thin covering near one's feet is also presented in the cognate noun מַטְמוֹן, which mostly signifies treasure or stores hidden underground, but little removed from discovery; see Jerem. 41 : 8; Prov. 2 : 4; Job 3 : 21; Isaiah 45 : 3; Gen. 43 : 23.

b. Regarding the meaning and use of צָפַן, a few points are to be observed. (1) The proper and usual sense of the word is not so much to 'hide' or 'conceal,' as rather simply to preserve, reserve, lay up or keep in store,—sometimes to retain or restrain. (2) More specifically, the term signifies to keep or preserve an object *near* at hand, and bestow on it particular care and attention. With this development of meaning, the value or preciousness of the object

---

[1] See the remarks already made regarding this word, at page 60.

hidden may come into greater distinctness or prominence. But the notion of proximity forms an important and very constant element. (3) The sense of hiding or concealment, sometimes undoubtedly attached to the word, appears at the most to be merely derivative and secondary or subordinate. The simplest and primary meaning is evident in such passages as Job 21 : 19, where it is said of the wicked, 'God reserveth (יִצְפֹּן) his iniquity [or, affliction] for his children ;' Prov. 2 : 7, where it is stated regarding Jehovah, ' He reserveth (יִצְפֹּן) aid for the upright [ones]; he is a shield to those who walk in integrity.' These instances throw light on other passages which in themselves are more obscure, as Hosea 13 : 12, 'The iniquity of Ephraim is bound up (צָרוּר), his sin is laid up'[1] (צְפוּנָה, i. e. reserved for future retribution); Ps. 56 : 6, where the writer says of his enemies, 'They gather themselves together, they store up [their] wrath ([2] יִצְפְּנוּ חֵמָה); my steps they mark, just as they have waited for my soul;' Job 15 : 20, '[During] all the days of a wicked man, he writhes in pain ; and [during] the number of the years [that] are reserved (נִצְפְּנוּ) to the tyrant, a voice of terror [is] in his ears.' Guidance is also afforded in the interpretation of a somewhat difficult passage, Pr. 27 : 15, 16, 'Constant dropping in a day of much rain, and a contentious woman, are alike. Every one who restraineth her restraineth the wind (צֹפְנֶיהָ צָפַן רוּחַ [3]), while his right hand encountereth oil.'

Specially instructive and important for our purpose are the instances in which the keeping or preserving has an intimate relation to *one's self*. Thus, Cant. 7 : 13, 'At our doors are all manner of precious [fruits], both new and old, my love, [which] I have reserved (צָפַנְתִּי) for thee;' Ps. 31 : 20, 'How great is thy goodness which thou hast laid up in store (צָפַנְתָּ) for those who fear thee!' Prov. 7 :1, 'My son, keep my words, and lay up (תִּצְפֹּן) my commandments with thee' (cf. also 2 : 1); Psalm 119 : 11, 'In my heart have I laid up (צָפַנְתִּי) thy word;' Job 10 : 13, 'These things hast thou laid up

---

[1] The rendering 'hid,' in the Authorised Version, is manifestly infelicitous.
[2] This reading seems preferable to that in the Massoretic text, יִצְפֹּנוּ הֵמָּה, which many expositors, in violation of grammatical principles, have been misled to interpret 'they hide themselves.'
[3] On the peculiar construction here employed, see the author's Introduction to Biblical Hebrew, 213, I, 2 e, or Davidson's Hebrew Syntax, page 160.

(צְפָנְתָּ) in thine heart;' Proverbs 10:14, 'Wise men store up (יִצְפְּנוּ) knowledge;' Psalm 17:14, 'With thy reserved [store] (וּצְפוּנְךָ) thou fillest their belly.' From these passages, in which צפן can scarcely signify quite to 'hide' or 'conceal,' it seems safe to infer that we must similarly render the somewhat obscure expression in Job 20:26 כָּל־חֹשֶׁךְ טָמוּן לִצְפּוּנָיו 'all kinds of hidden[1] darkness are certainly in store for him.' Psalm 83:4, 'Against thy people they take crafty counsel, and consult together against thy preserved [ones] (צְפוּנֶיךָ). See also Ezek. 7:22.

In some few instances, however, צפן does present an advance in meaning from mere careful preservation or safe-keeping to that of hiding from danger; the distinguishing feature of such concealment is that the object hidden is always *near* the concealer. Ps. 27:5 probably presents a transitional instance: here the Psalmist, after expressing his desire to abide all the days of his life in the house of God, that he might behold the beauty of the Lord and enquire in his temple, adds as his reason, 'For he shall preserve me [or, hide me,—near himself] (יִצְפְּנֵנִי) in his pavilion in the day of evil.'

An excellent illustration is found in the early history of Moses. In Ex. 2:2 we read that when Jochebed saw her infant son was a promising child, 'then she hid him (וַתִּצְפְּנֵהוּ) [near herself] for three months.' But when 'she could no longer hide him (הַצְּפִינוֹ) [beside her],' she took steps for exposing him by the side of the Nile, yet with careful precautions for his safety. And again, in Joshua 2:4 we find it is related of Rahab that when the king of Jericho sent messengers to seize the spies in her house, 'she took the two men and hid them (וַתִּצְפְּנוֹ) [near herself].'

Seeing that, in the passages just considered, צפן has a transitive force, perhaps the simplest mode of explaining Prov. 1:11, 18 and Ps. 10:8, where no direct object is expressly mentioned, is to supply an appropriate accusative, rather than assume a somewhat different and intransitive meaning (as 'lie in wait') for this verb; thus Pr. 1:11, 'Let us lie in ambush (נֶאֶרְבָה) for blood, let us store up (נִצְפְּנָה) [mischief] for the innocent;' verse 18, 'They lie in ambush for their own blood, they store up (יִצְפְּנוּ) [mischief] for their own lives;' Ps. 10:8, 'He murders the innocent, his eyes store up (יִצְפְּנוּ) [mischief] for the helpless.'

---

[1] For the distinctive meaning of טָמוּן, see what has been stated at page 66.

VERBS SIGNIFYING TO HIDE, CONCEAL.

c. The leading ideas associated with the root סתר are (1) mere *removal to a distance*, so that (2) the person or thing removed is out of sight ; hence the word is often naturally followed by such additions as 'from the eyes of,' 'from the face of,' 'from before,' etc. Further, (3) this invisibility is merely relative or partial, i. e. the object removed, though no longer seen by some, is not invisible to others. (4) The notion of intentional concealment is not primary, but has nevertheless become predominant; yet (5) the hiding is not necessarily effected by means of a covering laid upon the object, or through its being put in a covered spot : the invisibility is usually due to something which simply intervenes. Moreover (6) the concealment is mostly that of persons—not so frequently of material things—and still less that of conduct[1] or action : and again, (7) the hiding may be prompted by a sense of danger, whether actual or feared ; sometimes, however, it is an indication of displeasure towards the person from whom the withdrawal is made. These peculiarities we will now illustrate.

The primary sense somewhat rarely appears, but a clear case is found in the parting words of Laban to Jacob, Gen. 31 : 49, 'May Jehovah watch between me and thee, when we shall be hidden[2] (נִסָּתֵר) one from the other.' This hiding, however, was not the result of any effort or design[3] on either side ; it was but the natural and necessary consequence of Jacob's departure from Paddan-aram where Laban remained. Each was 'hidden' from the view of the other, but this merely by what intervened.

Similarly instructive is the force of the cognate noun סֵתֶר in 1 Sam. 25 : 20, where we read regarding Abigail that 'while she was riding on the ass, and coming down by a hidden part of the mountain (בְּסֵתֶר הָהָר)—and behold, David and his men were coming down in the opposite direction—she suddenly met them.' But this 'hidden part[4] of the mountain' was obviously not a spot deliberately chosen for concealment from David ; it was merely a part of the hillside, some distance off, down which any one—or even a considerable number of persons—might descend unobserved by others on

---

[1] As in the case of עָלַם, which is to be considered immediately.
[2] The rendering of the English Version, 'absent,' is rather mild.
[3] Contrast the use of חָבָא (soon to be elucidated) in verse 27.
[4] The common English rendering, 'covert,' is erroneous and misleading.

the opposite side, through the intervention of some natural screen, obstructing the view.

It still remains true, however, that the vast majority of passages in which derivatives from the root סתר are employed, present the idea of intentional concealment through removal to a distance. Let us first of all cite some instances in which the Niphal of the verb is found.

The very earliest illustration in the Hebrew Scriptures (Gen. 4 : 14) forms an excellent example. We read that Cain, complaining of the punishment laid on him by the Lord, exclaims, 'Behold, thou hast driven me out this day from the face of the ground, and from thy face shall I be hid (מִפָּנֶיךָ אֶסָּתֵר)...So Cain went out from before the face of (מִלִּפְנֵי) Jehovah.' Again, when David was forced to flee from Saul, he said to Jonathan, 'Let me go, and I shall hide myself (וְנִסְתַּרְתִּי) in the field' (בַּשָּׂדֶה) 1 Sam. 20 : 5 ; see also verses 19, 24. Once more, after predicting the famine sent on the land, because of the apostasy and idolatry of king and people, there came from the Lord the command to Elijah (1 Kings 17 : 3), 'Get thee hence......and hide thyself (וְנִסְתַּרְתָּ) in the valley [1] of the Cherith.' In all these cases, the 'hiding' consisted simply in withdrawal to a distance ; nor was the concealment complete, inasmuch as those hiding were at least visible—if not actually seen—by others in the region to which they had withdrawn, and there was no entering into a covered hiding-place such as a house or cave.[2] Similar withdrawal to a safe distance is indicated in the command to Baruch, Jer. 36 : 19, 'Go, hide thyself (הִסָּתֵר), thou and Jeremiah, and let no man know where ye are.'

Confirmatory illustrations are Prov. 22 : 3 (with its equivalent in 27 : 12), 'A prudent man seeth evil and hideth himself (וְנִסְתָּר), but simple people pass on, and pay the penalty.' Particularly instructive is Jer. 23 : 23, 24, 'Am I a God at hand, saith Jehovah, and not a God far off ? Can any one hide himself [by withdrawal] (יִסָּתֵר) in remote hiding-places (בַּמִּסְתָּרִים), so that I shall not see him ? declareth Jehovah. Do not I fill the heavens and the earth?' Similar corroboration is afforded by Ps. 19 : 7, where it is said of

---

[1] On the proper meaning of נַחַל in this passage, see the remarks in a later discussion on words signifying a 'river.'

[2] Contrast the meanings of צָפַן, טָמַן and חָבָא in this respect.

VERBS SIGNIFYING TO HIDE, CONCEAL.

the sun, 'his going forth is from one end of the heaven, and his circuit unto the end of it, and there is nothing hidden (נִסְתָּר) from [i. e. beyond the range of] his heat.' See also Deut. 7 : 20 ; Zeph. 2 : 3 ; Isaiah 40 : 27 ; 65 : 16.

The active verb-forms (סַתֵּר, הִסְתִּיר) afford further evidence of the meaning already established. In Isaiah 16 : 3, 4, the prophet, viewing Moab in the distance as an asylum for exiles, thus addresses the kindred nation : 'Hide (סַתְּרִי) the outcasts, discover not the wandering fugitive (נוֹדֵד[1]) ; be thou a distant place of hiding (סֵתֶר) unto them from the face of the spoiler;' once more it is obvious that those who were 'hidden' in the distance from their foes could yet at the same time be visible to their protectors. And when we next consider the numerous passages in which mention is made— especially in relation to God—of 'hiding the face' (הִסְתִּיר פָּנִים), we may at once perceive that the expression must ever be understood to mean withdrawal. Thus, in Deut. 31 : 17, 18, the Lord through Moses gives forewarning of the punishment to fall upon apostate Israel, ' I will forsake them and hide my face (וְהִסְתַּרְתִּי פָנַי) from them...so that it shall be said in that day, Is it not because my God is not with me [that] these evils have come upon me ? But I will assuredly hide my face (הַסְתֵּר אַסְתִּיר פָּנַי) in that day.' The language and spirit of Psalm 69 : 17-19 are likewise highly significant : 'Turn unto me...Hide not thy face (אַל־תַּסְתֵּר פָּנֶיךָ) from thy servant...Draw nigh unto my soul.' Other passages which may merely be quoted are Isa. 59 : 2, ' Your iniquities have been making separation between you and your God, and your sins have hidden [his] face (הִסְתִּירוּ פָנִים) from you, so that he does not hear ; ' Ps. 27 : 9, 'Hide not thy face from me ; turn not away thy servant in anger ; thou hast been my help ; leave me not, neither forsake me, O God of my salvation ;' Ps. 88 : 15, 'Lord, why dost thou cast off (תִּזְנַח) my soul ? [why] dost thou hide thy face from me ?' Specially noteworthy are two verses in the address of Elihu to Job (34 : 22, 29) regarding God : 'There is no darkness nor shadow of death whither workers of iniquity [may go] to hide themselves (לְהִסָּתֶר)...When he hideth his face (יַסְתֵּר פָּנִים) who can descry him (מִי יְשׁוּרֶנּוּ[2]) ?'

---

[1] See the remarks already made (page 6) on the meaning of this term.
[2] The verb שׁוּר signifies 'to look at objects *far off ;*' see Numbers 23 : 9 ; 24 : 17 ; Job 24 : 15 ; Cant. 4 : 8 ; Jer. 5 : 26 ; Hos. 13 : 7.

The results already obtained serve to correct a false impression generally prevalent regarding the meaning of the statement in Ex. 3 : 6, that when Jehovah had revealed himself at the burning bush, Moses 'hid his face (הִסְתִּיר פָּנָיו), for he was afraid to look upon God;' the 'hiding' was not covering. We are further enabled to perceive more precisely the sense of certain other passages. Thus Ps. 31 : 20, 21, 'How great is thy goodness which thou hast reserved [or 'hid' beside thee] (צָפַנְתָּ) for those who fear thee, [which] thou hast wrought for those who trust in thee before the sons of men ! Thou shalt [by removing] hide them (תַּסְתִּירֵם) in the [distant and] secret [place] of thy presence (סֵתֶר פָּנֶיךָ) from the plottings of man; thou shalt preserve [or 'hide'] them [near thee] (תִּצְפְּנֵם) in a tabernacle from the strife of tongues.' Consider also Jer. 16 : 17, 'Mine eyes [are] upon all their ways; they are not hidden [at a distance] from before my face (נִסְתְּרוּ מִלְּפָנַי), neither is their iniquity concealed [at hand] (נִצְפַּן) from before mine eyes.' Light is likewise shed on Job 14 : 13, 'O that thou wouldest hide me [near thee] in Sheol (מִי יִתֵּן בִּשְׁאוֹל תַּצְפִּנֵנִי)[1], that thou wouldest hide me [by removal to a distance] (תַּסְתִּירֵנִי) until thy wrath pass!' Some obscurity moreover is removed from the meaning of the nouns in Isa. 45 : 3, 'I will give unto thee treasures of darkness, and underground hidden stores in distant places (מַטְמֻנֵי מִסְתָּרִים).' Perhaps the greatest help however is afforded in reading Psalm 64 : 3, 'Hide me [at a distance] (תַּסְתִּירֵנִי) from the secret counsel of evil-doers who...have pointed their arrows...to shoot in [distant] hiding-places (מִסְתָּרִים) at an upright man...They speak of hiding (לִטְמוֹן) snares [on the ground]; they say, Who will see them ? '

d. With the general meaning of hiding or concealment, עָלַם associates, as its distinguishing feature, a reference to *actions* rather than to material things. While the term thus applies to persons, it mainly regards their *conduct* or behaviour. Actual examples of its employment will best elucidate these remarks.

A suitable opening for our investigations is presented by the cognate noun תַּעֲלֻמָה. Ps. 44 : 21, 22 runs thus, 'If we have for-

---

[1] Regarding this and alternative constructions, see Ewald's Hebrew Syntax, 329 c.; Gesenius' Hebrew Grammar (recent editions), 151 ; Davidson's Hebrew Syntax, 135; or the author's Introduction to Biblical Hebrew, 203 *Rem.*

VERBS SIGNIFYING TO HIDE, CONCEAL.

gotten the name of our God, and stretched out our hands unto a strange god, shall not God search this out? For *he* knoweth the secret workings (תַּעֲלֻמוֹת) of the heart.' And Zophar thus severely condemns Job (11 : 5-8) for daring to review the doings of the Almighty, 'O that God would speak and open his lips with thee, and declare unto thee the hidden workings of wisdom (תַּעֲלֻמוֹת חָכְמָה)... Canst thou attain unto the searching of God, or reach unto the perfection of the Almighty?' In both of these cases, the reference is to *hidden operations* carried on by sentient minds.

The general applicability of the verb עָלַם to concealed action, whether morally good, bad, or indifferent, is clearly seen in various passages. When the bereaved Shunammite woman had cast herself in her sorrow at the feet of Elisha, the prophet said to his servant Gehazi (2 Kings 4 : 27), 'Let her alone, for her soul is in bitterness, and the Lord hath hid (הֶעְלִים) [his doings] from me.' When the queen of Sheba visited Solomon, 'he told her all her affairs; there was nothing hidden (נֶעְלָם) from the king which he did not tell her (1 Kings 10 : 3; 2 Chr. 9 : 2). And the Preacher (Eccles. 12 : 14) concludes his meditations with the solemn reminder, 'Every work shall God bring into judgment, in addition to every hidden [deed] (נֶעְלָם), whether good or bad.'

More frequently, however, עָלַם refers to the commission of secret sins; thus Ps. 90 : 8, 'Thou hast placed our iniquities before thee, our hidden [sin] (עֲלֻמֵנוּ) in the light of thy countenance;' and similarly Psalm 26 : 4, 'I have not sat with wicked men, neither do I go with those who conceal themselves (נַעֲלָמִים) [in their evil ways].' The term accordingly finds appropriate employment when reference is made in the law of Moses to the unconscious commission of sin. Thus we read in Leviticus 4 : 13-21 the requirements to be fulfilled whenever 'the whole congregation of Israel should inadvertently commit sin (יִשְׁגּוּ) and the matter be hid (נֶעְלַם) from the eyes of the assembly' (v. 13). In like manner, the term is properly introduced in three consecutive verses of the succeeding chapter (Lev. 5 : 2-4) where a general account is given of the different ways in which a man might possibly incur sin, that might nevertheless be 'hidden' (נֶעְלַם) from him.

The radical idea inherent in the verb reveals itself distinctly in the Hiphil and Hithpaël forms. To 'hide the eyes' (הֶעְלִים עֵינַיִם),

or the ear, or to 'hide one's self' (הִתְעַלֵּם) then essentially signifies to *refrain from action*, especially when active assistance seems urgently required. Thus, the Lord declared through Isaiah (1:15) to sinful Israel, 'When ye stretch forth your hands [in prayer for help], I will hide mine eyes (אַעְלִים עֵינַי) from you.' The meaning is quite obvious in such passages as Prov. 28:27, 'He that giveth to a [hungry] poor man ([1]רָשׁ) hath no lack, but he that hideth his eyes (מַעְלִים עֵינָיו) hath plenty of curses;' Lam. 3:56, 'My voice hast thou heard: hide not thine ear (אַל־תַּעְלֵם אָזְנְךָ);' Psalm 10:1, 'Lord, why dost thou stand afar off? [why] dost thou hide ([2]תַּעְלִים) [thine eyes] in times of trouble?' Divine judgments are threatened in Levit. 20:4, 5, 'if the people of the land should wholly hide (הַעְלֵם יַעְלִימוּ) their eyes' from any man when he gave any of his seed to Molech, and did not kill him. The prophet Samuel, feeling constrained in his old age to call the attention of the people to his strict integrity and impartiality as a judge, significantly asks them (1 Sam. 12:3), 'From whose hand have I taken a bribe, that I might hide mine eyes (אַעְלִים עֵינַי) therewith?' On the other hand, the Lord had to complain through Ezekiel (22:26) regarding the priests, 'From my sabbaths have they hidden their eyes, and I am profaned among them.'

Passages in which the Hithpaël is employed are Isaiah 58:7, 'From thine own flesh thou shalt not hide thyself' (לֹא תִתְעַלָּם); Ps. 55:2, 'Give ear, O God, unto my prayer, and hide not thyself from my supplication;' Deut. 22:1-4, 'Thou shalt not see thy brother's ox or his sheep going astray, and hide thyself (וְהִתְעַלַּמְתָּ) from them ...And so shalt thou do unto his ass; ...thou shalt not be at liberty to hide thyself (לְהִתְעַלֵּם). Thou shalt not see thy brother's ox or his ass fallen down in the way, and hide thyself from them.'

The conclusions now reached enable us to understand two passages more clearly than would have been possible without such results. Job 28:20, 21 runs thus:— 'But wisdom,—whence does it come? and where is the place of understanding? seeing it is concealed [in

---

[1] See the later chapter on words meaning 'poor.'

[2] The usage already explained, as well as the form of the verb itself, forbids us to render this word reflexively ('hide thyself'). Other terms in this Psalm (verse 8), signifying to 'hide' have already been discussed, at page 70.

its workings] (נֶעְלְמָה) from the eyes of all living, and is hidden [at a distance] (נִסְתְּרָה) from the fowls of heaven.'

Num. 5 : 13 may also be read now with a feeling of confidence. This verse occurs in a passage giving legislative directions regarding an adulteress, 'when a man had lain with her...and it [viz. the sinful deed] had been hidden (נֶעְלַם) from the eyes of her husband, and she had hidden [i. e. withdrawn] herself (נִסְתְּרָה), seeing that[1] she was defiled (וְהִיא נִטְמָאָה), and there was no witness against her inasmuch as[1] she had not been seized [in the act]' (וְהִוא לֹא נִתְפָּשָׂה). From what we have now seen, it follows that נֶעְלַם can only refer to the sin as an *act*, whereas נִסְתְּרָה points to the *self-seclusion* of the faithless wife.

e. Regarding חָבָא and the rarer cognate form חָבָה, it is to be observed (1) that the hiding they indicate nearly always[2] applies to *persons*, not to material things or to actions ; (2) that the concealment is prompted by strong *fear* of actual or possible danger ; (3) that removal by flight to a distance is not necessarily involved ; (4) that the concealment is thorough ; and (5) that some kind of covering overhead, or place of refuge within a limited area—such as a house, or a cave, or a wood—is almost always understood, if not actually mentioned. In these last three respects particularly, חָבָא and חָבָה obviously differ from הִסְתִּיר.

An early chapter in Genesis (3 : 8-10) affords a good illustration. Adam and Eve, after they had sinned, 'heard the voice of the Lord God,...and Adam and his wife hid themselves (הִתְחַבְּאוּ) from the face of the Lord God among the trees of the garden ;' and when called, Adam answered, 'I was afraid, because I was naked, and I hid myself (וָאֵחָבֵא).' In the Book of Joshua (10 : 16, 17, 27) we read that the five defeated Amorite kings 'fled and hid themselves (וַיֵּחָבְאוּ) in a cave in Makkedah. And it was told Joshua, saying, The five kings are found hid (נֶחְבְּאִים) in a cave in Makkedah.' The conqueror, stopping merely to make a temporary prison of the cave, by rolling huge stones to its mouth, afterwards returned to

---

[1] The force of the 'circumstantial clauses' must be carefully observed. On such constructions, see Driver on the Hebrew Tenses, 160 ; Davidson's Hebrew Syntax, 137 ; or the author's Introduction to Biblical Hebrew, 229, I.

[2] Exceptions are found in Job 38 : 30 ; 29 : 10.

execute the prisoners, whose bodies were then cast 'into the cave where they had hid themselves' (נֶחְבְּאוּ). Later, in Jud. 9 : 5, we note the brief remark that although Abimelech, the son of Gideon, fancied he had slain all his brethren, who certainly, if left alive, would at once have disputed his usurped authority, yet Jotham the youngest escaped, 'for he had hid himself' (נֶחְבָּא). Saul, already knowing that the lot in the public election of a king would fall on him, 'hid himself (נֶחְבָּא) among the stuff' (1 Sam. 10 : 22). Not long after, we read (1 Sam. 13 : 6) that when the Philistines advanced in force against the Israelites, the people were afraid, 'and they hid themselves (וַיִּתְחַבְּאוּ) in caves' and other similar places of concealment, so that, when the brave Jonathan and his armour-bearer attacked their enemies, these sneeringly cried out, 'Behold, the Hebrews are coming out of the holes where they have been hiding themselves (הִתְחַבְּאוּ).' With a show of caution, Hushai presses the insurgent Absalom to consider how it is more than probable that his father David (2 Sam. 17 : 9) was 'hid (נֶחְבָּא) in one of the pits' and might suddenly give renewed proof of his old valour. Risking everything, the God-fearing Obadiah, Ahab's servant, took an hundred prophets of Jehovah 'and hid them (וַיַּחְבִּיאֵם) by fifty in a cave' (1 Kings 18 : 4, cf. also ver. 13). In the Book of Daniel (10 : 7) it is recorded regarding the men who were with the seer when he had one of his visions, that 'a great fear fell upon them, and they fled [secretly [1]] to hide themselves' (וַיִּבְרְחוּ בְּהֵחָבֵא). For further illustrations, see 1 Chr. 21 : 20 ; 2 Kings 6 : 29 ; 7 : 12 ; 1 Kings 22 : 25 (2 Chr. 18 : 24) ; Isa. 26 : 20 ; 42 : 22 ; Job 5 : 21 ; 29 : 8.

Let us apply the results now ascertained to other passages, in which the distinction between different terms must be carefully observed.

It is recorded of Rahab in the Book of Joshua (2 : 4) that when the king of Jericho sent his messengers to seize the spies, she 'took the two men and hid them (וַתִּצְפְּנוֹ);' the verb here employed, as we have already seen, points mainly to the care and interest she displayed in preserving them safely near herself. Reaching verse 6, where it is stated that she afterwards 'brought them up to the roof, and hid them (וַתִּטְמְנֵם) with stalks of flax,' we perceive that the term

---

[1] See the remarks made at page 3.

VERBS SIGNIFYING TO HIDE, CONCEAL.   79

now introduced points to an effective and complete though superficial concealment at the level on which one walks. But when we come to verse 16, we find her urging the men to seek safety in instant flight : 'Get ye to the mountain, lest the pursuers come upon you, and hide yourselves (וְנַחְבֵּתֶם) there for three days;' the employment of this last verb, as we have seen, adds new and stronger elements to the notion of concealment. It is noteworthy that when reference is afterwards made (Josh. 6 : 17, 25) to the fact that Rahab 'hid the messengers,' the writer selects the verb which conveys the strongest meaning (הֶחְבִּיאָה, הֶחְבָּאתָה).

In reading the history of David, it becomes necessary to mark carefully the transition from one to another of the terms now explained. Then we may perceive a distinct gradation in the words of Jonathan to David, recorded in 1 Sam. 19 : 2, 'Saul my father seeketh to kill thee; now therefore, do take care of thyself in the morning, and abide in a [distant] hiding-place (בַּסֵּתֶר), and conceal thyself closely (וְנַחְבֵּאתָ) [in a covered place].' Still more striking is the selection of terms employed later, in the account of a particular episode in David's wilderness-life. Ziphites came to Saul at Gibeah and said, 'Is not David hiding himself [from thee] (מִסְתַּתֵּר) with us?...Now therefore...come down' (1 Sam. 23 : 19). The messengers mean that though distance hides David from Saul, the fugitive is not unseen by them, but moves about somewhat freely. On the other hand, when Saul gladly accepts their offer to betray David, he requests them carefully to mark 'all the hiding-places (מַחֲבֹאִים) where he conceals himself' (יִתְחַבֵּא) before they bring back word to him again. Another kind of hiding is before the mind of Saul.

Again, when Athaliah usurped the throne after the death of her son Ahaziah (2 Kings 11 : 1-3 ; cf. 2 Chr. 22 : 9-12), she sought to secure her position by exterminating all possible opponents. But Joash, a youthful son of Ahaziah, was saved by his aunt Jehoshebah, 'and they hid (וַיַּסְתִּרוּ) him [by removing him] from the face of Athaliah. And he was with her [viz. his aunt] in the house of the Lord, concealing himself completely (מִתְחַבֵּא) for six years, while Athaliah reigned over the land.' Something more than change of terms is here involved.

Job 31 : 33 receives elucidation from what has previously been established. According to the Masoretes and most expositors, the protesting sufferer contends thus, 'If, like Adam,[1] I have covered my transgressions, by concealing mine iniquity in my bosom (לְמְמוֹן בְּחֻבִּי עֲוֹנִי), because I fear a great multitude, and the contempt of families terrifies me, so that I kept silence and went not out at the door...' We have already shown that טָמַן properly refers to something hidden on or near the ground ; hence בחבי surely cannot mean 'in *my bosom.*' It turns out that this interpretation is merely conjectural at best ; the supposed noun חֹב is said to be derived, with a secondary meaning, from the verb חָבַב (only once found, in Deut. 33 : 3, although the cognate form is common in Aramaic). On the other hand, it seems much more natural to assume a form חַבִּי (from the verb חָבָה)with the idea of complete concealment overhead, as already explained ; the entire form would then be בְּחַבִּי (for בְּבַחֲבִי), and this might then be rendered 'as in a completely covered hiding-place.' Such a reading, with its corresponding interpretation, further receives confirmation from verse 34, but particularly its closing words, 'I kept still, and went not out at the door.'

---

[1] This rendering of כְּאָדָם is certainly more lucid and appropriate than that of some expositors whose translation, 'like a man,' is rather vague ; cf. Hosea 6 : 7. Reference to Adam, by recalling the story of the Fall, further confirms the proposed change to בְּחַבִּי, the very form of which distinctly points to the peculiar terms employed (Gen. 3 : 8, 10) in mentioning the hiding of the guilty pair ; see page 77.

13. Adjectives signifying Poor.

a. אֶבְיוֹן   b. דַּל   c. מִסְכֵּן

d. רָאשׁ, רָשׁ.[1]

As the Hebrew language possesses a considerable number of words bearing in common the idea of poverty, some difficulty is experienced in translating each into English. On the other hand, it is remarkable that no Hebrew equivalent is found for what we call a 'pauper,' and a 'sturdy beggar' is equally unknown. But such beings are perhaps to be regarded as products of our later and more complex civilisation.

a. With the essential notion of poverty, and this (1) in a high degree,[2] אֶבְיוֹן conjoins the idea of (2) helplessness, and (3) more or less of permanence or constancy in want. In other words, this term designates one who is deficient in internal as well as external resource. With the lack of material possessions there is associated a want of independence, so that we find, in one form or another, constant reference to assistance on the part of others. Thus the אֶבְיוֹן means one who is weak in will as well as wanting in worldly wealth. In his case, 'pride and poverty' are *not* combined; he does not scorn relief when it is offered; frequently, indeed, he looks for it, and does not scruple to confess his poverty, to cry for help.

---

[1] It may be observed that no place has been assigned in this group to the term עָנִי in which, though the idea of poverty is sometimes distinctly presented (see Ex. 22:24; Deut. 24:12, etc.), the element of wretchedness vastly preponderates.

[2] Compare in this respect the meanings severally attached to דַּל and רָשׁ.

A few simple illustrations may be cited. In Deut. 15 : 7-11, the duty of the rich to the deserving but helpless poor is thus enforced: 'When there shall be among you a poor man (אֶבְיוֹן) of one of thy brethren in one of thy gates..., thou shalt not harden thine heart, neither shalt thou shut up thine hand from thy poor [and helpless] brother (אָחִיךָ הָאֶבְיוֹן), but thou shalt by all means open thine hand to him. For a poor [and helpless person] (אֶבְיוֹן) shall not fail from the midst of the land; therefore do I command thee, saying, Thou shalt by all means open thine hand to thy brother, to thy wretched ones and to thy poor (לַעֲנִיֶּךָ וּלְאֶבְיֹנְךָ) in thy land.' Similarly, in Deut. 24 : 14 the admonition is enforced, 'Thou shalt not oppress a wretched and poor hireling, [whether one] of thy brethren or of thy strangers who are in thy land, within thy gates.' Job (29 : 16) in self-defence protests, 'I was a father to the poor' (לָאֶבְיוֹנִים), and he afterwards asks, in similar strains (Job 30 : 25), 'Did not...my soul grieve for the poor (לְאֶבְיוֹן)?' In Ps. 112 : 9 it is said to the praise of the good and godly man that 'he hath dispersed, he hath given to the poor' (לָאֶבְיוֹנִים); and in Prov. 31 : 20 of the excellent woman that 'she spreadeth out her palm to the wretched (לֶעָנִי), and reacheth forth her hands to the poor' (לָאֶבְיוֹן); while the Lord's promise in Ps. 132 : 15 regarding Zion is, 'her poor ones (אֶבְיוֹנֶיהָ) will I satisfy with bread.'

Further illustrations of acknowledged poverty combined with petition for relief are frequent in the Psalms. 'Though I am miserable and [helplessly] poor (עָנִי וְאֶבְיוֹן), yet the Lord thinketh on me; thou art my help and my deliverer; O my God, do not tarry' (40: 18); 'Though I am wretched and helplessly poor (עָנִי וְאֶבְיוֹן), O God, make haste to me; thou art my help and my deliverer; O Lord, tarry not' (70 : 6); 'Incline thine ear, O Lord; hear and answer me, for I am wretched and [helplessly] poor' (86 : 1); 'Because thy mercy is good, deliver thou me; for I am wretched and [helplessly] poor, and my heart is wounded within me' (Ps. 109 : 21, 22, see also 69 : 34).

But the idea of helplessness or defencelessness, superadded to that of deep and constant poverty, becomes specially prominent in those passages—and they are somewhat numerous—which speak of justice for the needy. 'Thou shalt not wrest the judgment of thy poor (מִשְׁפַּט אֶבְיֹנְךָ) in his cause' is the solemn warning given in the

Mosaic law (Ex. 23 : 6). There is the assurance in Ps. 9 : 19, 'A poor man shall not always be forgotten;' similarly, the Almighty declares in Ps. 12 : 6, 'Because of the oppression of the wretched, because of the groaning of the poor (אֶנְקַת אֶבְיוֹנִים), now will I arise;' and in Psalm 69 : 34 we read the comforting reminder, 'The Lord listeneth to poor ones (אֶל־אֶבְיוֹנִים), and his prisoners he despiseth not.' Specially instructive are the Psalmist's confident words of praise for his Lord (Ps. 109 : 31), 'He shall stand at the right hand of the poor (אֶבְיוֹן), to save [him] from those who judge his soul;' and similarly in 140 : 13, 'I know that the Lord will maintain the cause of the wretched, the right of the poor' (מִשְׁפַּט אֶבְיוֹנִים); and one of Lemuel's exhortations to his son, in Prov. 31 : 9, is, 'Open thy mouth, judge [in] righteousness, and defend the cause of the wretched and poor.'

Defence of the helpless poor in their just cause becomes even more distinctly visible, perhaps, in the writings of certain prophets; thus Isa. 29 : 19 f., 'The poor among men (אֶבְיוֹנֵי אָדָם) shall rejoice in the Holy One of Israel, for the terrible one is come to nought, and the scorner is come to an end, and all those who watch for iniquity are cut off;' Jer. 20 : 13, 'Praise ye the Lord, for he hath delivered the soul of the poor (נֶפֶשׁ אֶבְיוֹן) from the hand of evil-doers.' The same thing is evident from other passages in which injustice is denounced, as Ezekiel 18 : 12, 'The wretched and poor (עָנִי וְאֶבְיוֹן) hath he afflicted' (see a similar expression in 22 : 29); Amos 2 : 6, 'They sold a righteous man for silver, and a poor man (אֶבְיוֹן) for a pair of shoes;' 5 : 12, 'I know that your transgressions are many...taking a bribe, and turning aside poor ones (אֶבְיוֹנִים) in the gate;' 8 : 4, 'Hear this, O ye who pant after a poor [and helpless] man (אֶבְיוֹן).'

b. The varied use of דַּל shows very clearly that such a term as 'poverty' is largely relative. There are all degrees in poverty and wealth, as there are standards manifold and varying; nevertheless, comparison is possible, even when a changing standard is applied.

When used—as almost always[1] is the case—with reference to wealth, דַּל does not bear the vague sense 'poor,' but more precisely

---

[1] In Gen. 41 : 19 and 2 Sam. 13 : 4, the term is applied to decline in bodily health and condition,—extreme emaciation.

signifies (1) 'impoverished,' reduced in means. Thus it refers, by implication, to a former state of greater affluence, from which descent has taken place; the thought of *loss* sustained by one who is described as דַּל is further emphasised through the occasional association of this term in certain passages (Job 31 : 16 ; Ps. 82 : 3) with יָתוֹם ('orphan'),—for, obviously, loss of wealth and loss of parents frequently combine. But (2) on the lower side, the fall is not into the deepest want, the direst poverty ; one who may be fitly classed as דַּל has still some property, and stands upon a higher level than another to whom אֶבְיוֹן properly applies. Further, (3) although a measure of discouragement is naturally found in one whose fortunes are diminished, he is not quite crushed in spirit; there is still some courage left. Accordingly, we rarely read (as in Prov. 21 : 13 ; Job 34 : 28) of any one 'impoverished' (דַּל) raising a 'cry' for help, as if his means and strength were gone.

Safe guidance in our inquiries is here afforded by the cognate verb דָּלַל which primarily signifies to 'hang down' from above, or to be let down; there is accordingly implicit or explicit reference to a superior position with which some kind of connection exists. Thus, in Psalm 79 : 8 are found the doleful words, 'We are brought down very low' (דַּלּוֹנוּ); and similarly in 142 : 7, 'Listen to my cry, for I am brought very low'(דַּלּוֹתִי מְאֹד); while in 116 : 6 there is grateful testimony borne to the Lord's deliverance, 'I was brought low (דַּלּוֹתִי), and he saved me.' Most directly valuable, however, for our purpose is the statement in Jud. 6 : 6, introductory to the account of Gideon's judgeship, that when the Midianites had made themselves masters of Israel, their hosts plundered or destroyed everything they could find, 'so that Israel was very much impoverished' (וַיִּדַּל יִשְׂרָאֵל מְאֹד). All of these passages indicate a change from comfort to discomfort, from sufficiency to insufficiency, a descent from wealth to want. But is this want complete and absolute, or merely partial?

A decisive answer to this question is contained in words used by the shrinking Gideon, when called to head his countrymen against the Midianites, 'Behold, my family is the most impoverished in Manasseh (הַדַּל בִּמְנַשֶּׁה), and I am the least in my father's house' (Jud. 6 : 15). 'The most impoverished' could not mean 'destitute.' For, when the heavenly messenger appeared and called the son of

Joash to expel the foreign ravagers (verse 11), he was engaged in threshing[1] wheat in the trough of the wine-press (גַּת); this circumstance alone surely proves anything but 'poverty' as usually understood. Moreover, no one absolutely poor could forthwith (ver. 19) have furnished 'a kid and an ephah of flour [in] unleavened cakes' for the honoured visitant. Still less does the fact that his father had at least two bullocks (ver. 27) and more than ten servants (ver. 27) show pressing want. The lack of wealth was merely relative; and Gideon, by using דַּל when speaking of his family, mainly intended to point out their circumstances as 'reduced,' that for this reason he might be excused. He certainly could not have rightly used the term אֶבְיוֹן in speaking of himself or of his family, though דַּל was quite appropriate.

This idea of change from better to worse is likewise distinctly present in the rarer use of דַּל to mark a growing weakness, as in 2 Sam. 3:1, where we read that 'while David grew stronger and stronger, the house of Saul grew feebler and feebler' (וְדַלִּים הֹלְכִים); and in the question asked by Jonadab at Amnon (2 Sam. 13:4), 'Why art thou, the king's son, so lean and weak (דַּל) from day to day?' there is implicit contrast drawn between Amnon's enfeebled state and what had been his wont.

Returning to consider other passages in which דַּל refers rather to wealth than health, we find that our conclusions are remarkably confirmed. Thus, when we read in the Mosaic law (Exod. 30:15) the injunction regarding the half-shekel to be paid by every person aged twenty years or over, 'The rich man shall not give more, and the impoverished one (הַדַּל) shall not give less than the half-shekel,' it is obviously implied that those whose fortunes were reduced had something still remaining and were not quite destitute; further, the essence of this ordinance is the fundamental principle that diminution of property could not be accepted as an excuse for diminution of payment. Still more clearly does the force of דַּל appear in the merciful modification of the law (Lev. 14:21 ff.) regulating the offerings to be brought by one who had been cured of leprosy;

---

[1] The employment here of חָבַט ('beating out' with a stick) instead of the usual דּוּשׁ ('treading out' under the threshing-wains or sledges, and the feet of the oxen which dragged these over the floor) forms one of the significant points in the narrative.

'If he be an impoverished person' (אִם דַּל הוּא)—doubtless a common and natural result of exclusion from the society of others—'then he shall take one lamb as a trespass-offering...' together with less costly accompaniments. Again, when the Hebrew sage (Prov. 19 : 4) records the patent truth that 'wealth makes many friends, while an impoverished one (דַּל) is separated from his friend,' the main point emphasised throughout is change of lot.

Again, when it is recorded (in Jer. 39 : 10) that while the mass of the Jewish nation was carried captive to Babylon, 'Nebuzaradan left in the land of Judah some of the people, the most impoverished (מִן־הָעָם הַדַּלִּים) who had nothing,' we are of course to understand that though their property was well-nigh gone, they still retained a self-reliant spirit. We may now perceive, too, reason for the choice of language made by Amos (2 : 7) in denouncing 'those who pant after the dust of the earth on the head of the impoverished' דַּלִּים ; these had already lost, at the oppressors' hands, almost everything they once possessed, but their tormentors would take even more, if that were possible.

We now seem also to have found a simple explanation of the prohibition in Ex. 23 : 3, 'An impoverished person (דַּל) thou shalt not countenance in his suit.' When there are many solemn warnings given against neglect or oppression of a [helplessly] poor man (אֶבְיוֹן) in his suit,[1] it might at first seem strange to find here an injunction not to *favour* an 'impoverished' person at the judgment-seat; should not the tendency seem all the other way? But when we think how much regard is often paid, through mere compassion, to one whose fortunes are decayed,—who has seen better days, and still retains his self-respect, or dignity of manner,—when we further bear in mind the swaying influence of personal friendship, such as might probably exist between a judge and one before him who had once been better off—we can perceive some reason for the caution *not* to make undue allowance at the judgment-bar for one who had become impoverished.

Further confirmation of what has been already ascertained regarding the precise meaning of דַּל is found in Job 20 : 10. The preceding context shows how evanescent is the joy of wicked men;

---

[1] See the quotations on pages 82, 83.

ADJECTIVES SIGNIFYING POOR.

then follows (v. 10) the assurance that 'his children shall conciliate impoverished ones (דַּלִּים), and his own hands shall restore (תָּשֵׁבְנָה) his substance.' But, in this case, to 'restore' is to give back what had iniquitously been taken from those who thereby became 'impoverished' in the way so graphically sketched (v. 19), 'he crushed, forsook [those whom he had made] impoverished' (דַּלִּים).

It is of importance also to note the verbs employed in Hebrew when reference is made to robbing the poor. 'He that violently defraudeth an impoverished person (עֹשֵׁק דָּל) reproacheth his Maker; but he that pitieth a destitute person (חֹנֵן אֶבְיוֹן) honoureth him' Prov. 14:31; 'He that violently defraudeth an impoverished person (עֹשֵׁק דָּל) to multiply [wealth] for himself...is surely [destined] for want,' Prov. 22:16; when in these passages and in Prov. 28:3 we find the verb employed is עָשַׁק, which signifies to defraud or rob with violence, the defrauded one (דָּל) must, of course, have something of which he could be deprived. This becomes more evident when we consider the distinction presented in Amos 4:1, 'Hear ye this word, O kine of Bashan, that are in the mountain of Samaria, that violently defraud impoverished ones (הָעֹשְׁקוֹת דַּלִּים), that crush destitute ones' (הָרֹצְצוֹת אֶבְיוֹנִים); those who were utterly destitute had nothing of which they could be robbed but liberty and life; their lot was thus maltreatment. The same prophet again (2:6, 7) affords another illustration, of a like contrast, in announcing woes to fall on the Israelites 'because they sold a righteous man (צַדִּיק) for silver, and a helplessly poor one (אֶבְיוֹן) for a pair of shoes; that pant after the dust of the earth on the head of impoverished ones' (דַּלִּים). From those of fallen fortunes, everything of even the slightest value must be snatched away,—the very dust upon their head; as for the destitute, helplessly poor (אֶבְיוֹנִים),—what could they offer as an object for rapacity? Only their persons. Even these, then, must be seized and sold for anything that they may bring—a pair of shoes.

Once more this prophet (Amos 8:4-6) sets before us the distinction between these two terms, אֶבְיוֹן and דָּל; 'Hear this, O ye that pant after a destitute person (אֶבְיוֹן)..., saying, when will the new moon be gone, that we may sell corn? and the sabbath, that we may open out grain..., to buy impoverished ones (דַּלִּים) for silver and a destitute one (אֶבְיוֹן) for a pair of shoes?' The difference in estimated value certainly involves a corresponding difference in rank and worth.

c. In determining the proper sense of מִסְכֵּן, we derive assistance from the cognate noun מִסְכֵּנוּת, although this meets us only once, in Deut. 8 : 9, where Canaan is declared to be for Israel 'a land in which thou shalt eat bread without scarceness' (לֹא בְמִסְכֵּנֻת). This term thus obviously points to stint—straitened circumstances wanting that margin which gives ease and even positive enjoyment in the use of means. The word at once suggests the need of care and forethought to 'make both ends meet;' just at this point is felt the 'pinch of poverty,' and 'carking care,' though utterly unwelcome, comes to stay.

The kindred Pual participle מְסֻכָּן leads us still further to the concrete, bringing us to view a person of straitened means but correspondingly increased thoughtfulness; to such a one, straitened circumstances prove a contant stimulus to active exercise of mental power. These points are visible in Isa. 40:20, the single passage where this form appears : 'He who has becomes straitened [as regards] a valuable offering (הַמְסֻכָּן תְּרוּמָה) chooses [for making an idol] a tree [that] will not rot.'

On coming now to מִסְכֵּן itself, we are prepared to find that this term signifies—not one in helpless, heartless poverty (אֶבְיוֹן), or one whose 'circumstances' are reduced (דַּל), but rather one who, though not positively needy, nevertheless (1) is limited in means, and (2) has his faculties particularly sharpened through the constant pressure of anxiety to make the best and most of what he actually has. Naturally, such a person will be, for the most part, also (3) self-reliant, independent, and will cherish self-respect.

These three features show themselves in the two passages in which the word occurs; thus Eccl. 4 : 13, 'Better is a lad of straitened means but wise (מִסְכֵּן וְחָכָם), than a king [who is] old and a garrulous fool ([1] זָקֵן וּכְסִיל), who no longer knows to take warning.' Consider also Eccl. 9 : 14, 'There was a little city, with a few men in it; and there came unto it a great king, and he besieged it and built against it vast mounds.[2] And there was found in it a man

---

[1] See the discussions on words signifying 'fool' (p. 29) and 'old' (p. 55).
[2] Here we read מְצוֹדִים instead of מְצוֹדִים as in the Masoretic text.

ADJECTIVES SIGNIFYING POOR. 89

of straitened means, a wise man (אִישׁ מִסְכֵּן חָכָם), and he by his wisdom delivered the city; yet nobody remembered that man of straitened means' (הָאִישׁ הַמִּסְכֵּן הַהוּא).

d. The term רָשׁ (properly the participle Qal of רוּשׁ, and sometimes found in the form רָאשׁ, Prov. 10:4; 13:23) possesses several noteworthy features, so far as regards its meaning and use. (1) It properly applies to one in deep poverty, and this, on the whole, not of a temporary character; (2) the special nature of the poverty it usually marks is want of food; nevertheless, (3) the person indicated is, in the main, a sturdy nature used to earn his living by his labour, and thus unaccustomed to cry out for help, or beg the bread he really may need. Sometimes, his strength of character makes him unlovely,—hard in himself and harsh to others, void of sympathy. The enduring nature of the want experienced by one described as רָשׁ will be sufficiently attested in the passages now to be cited; attention may rather, therefore, in the first instance, be directed to those in which the special feature of the poverty is a deficiency in the means of subsistence.

Somewhat remarkably, the only instance in which the Qal perfect of the verb רוּשׁ occurs is Psalm 34:11, where it is applied to creatures lower than man: 'Young lions are in want [of food] and suffer hunger (כְּפִירִים[1] רָשׁוּ וְרָעֵבוּ), but those who seek the Lord do not lack (לֹא־יַחְסְרוּ) any good.' Other passages distinctly referring to a stint of food as essentially constituting this kind of poverty are Prov. 13:23, 'Much food [is in the] cultivable land of hungry poor (נִיר רָאשִׁים), but it is actually swept away through unrighteousness.' Most decisive, however, on the special point now before us are some passages in which the cognate noun of state (רֵאשׁ or רִישׁ) is introduced; in these it is perfectly patent that the 'poverty' essentially consists in lack of the necessaries of life. In Prov. 28:19, let the antithesis be carefully noted, 'He that tilleth his land shall be satisfied with bread, whereas he that eagerly followeth vain persons shall be sated with poverty' (רִישׁ) [in the shape of want of food]. This is further confirmed by the whole spirit and language of the well-known address in Prov. 6:6-11, 'Go to the ant, O sluggard; consider her ways and be wise,—which, [though] having no leader,

---

[1] See the remarks already made at page 23, on words signifying 'lion.'

overseer, or ruler, [yet] in summer prepareth her bread, and in the harvest gathereth her food. How long, O sluggard, wilt thou lie [resting]? when wilt thou arise from thy sleep? A little [more] sleep,[1] a little slumber, a little folding of the hands to sleep,—and thy poverty [of provisions] (רֵאשֶׁךָ) shall come as a robber (מִתְהַלֵּךְ) and thy want (מַחְסֹרֶךָ) as an armed man.' (See the similar passage in Prov. 24 : 30-34, with identical conclusion). Additional proof is afforded by the terms of Agur's prayer, recorded in Prov. 30 : 8, 9, 'Give me not poverty or riches (רֵאשׁ וָעֹשֶׁר), feed me with my apportioned food (לֶחֶם חֻקִּי) ; lest I be satiated and deny [thee], and say, Who is the Lord? or lest I be reduced to [starvation] poverty (אִוָּרֵשׁ) and steal.' The kind of poverty he feared was, evidently, want of food.

The specific meaning of the adjective רָשׁ, as now determined, is further exhibited in the opening verses of Nathan's parable addressed to David (2 Sam. 12 : 1), 'There were two men in one city, one rich and another poor (רָאשׁ). The rich man had very many flocks and herds, but the poor man had nothing except one little ewe lamb, which he had bought and nourished ; and it grew up with him and his children together ; it ate of his morsel (מִפִּתּוֹ) and drank of his cup.' How appropriately is the food of one in his circumstances called a 'morsel!'

Turning now to that point in David's history when it was suggested that he should marry Michal, the daughter of Saul (1 Sam. 18 : 23), we find him answering the king's servants, 'Is it a light matter in your eyes to become the king's son-in-law, seeing that I am a poor man (אִישׁ־רָשׁ) and of small esteem?' In selecting the term רָשׁ to describe his condition generally, he meant to say that he could barely keep himself in food,—far less support a daughter of the king besides, in a becoming style.

In Eccl. 4 : 13, 14, we mark a striking change of terms : 'Better is a lad of straitened means but wise (יֶלֶד מִסְכֵּן וְחָכָם), than a king [who is] old and a garrulous fool.[2]...For out of the prison-house he cometh forth to reign, although in his own kingdom he was born poor' (רָשׁ) [with scanty fare]. This last term further here marks force of character.

---

[1] See the chapter on nouns signifying 'sleep,' pages 26, 27.
[2] This verse has been already cited on page 88.

ADJECTIVES SIGNIFYING POOR.

This leads us to remark that in some passages of the Old Testament the other element in רָשׁ comes into greater prominence,— a certain strength of mind which commonly displays itself in self-reliance, but may in some instances assume a harsh or unattractive form. Though, in a single passage (Prov. 18 : 23), it is said that such a poor man 'uttereth entreaties (תַּחֲנוּנִים), whereas a rich man answereth harshly,' there is no evidence to show he loses heart and hope even when oppressed, or that he condescends to beg. 'Better is a [scantily fed] poor man (רָשׁ) walking in his integrity, than one who is perverse in his ways, though he be rich' (Prov. 28 : 6 ; see a similar sentence in 19 : 1) ; 'A [scantily fed] poor man is better than a liar' (Prov. 19 : 22) ; such passages distinctly point to estimable firmness of character combined with poverty. A solitary instance (Prov. 28 : 3) shows how strong minds, through the dire experience of poverty, may ultimately lose the finer, nobler features of humanity : 'A strong man [who is] poor [in means of nourishment], and forcibly defrauds impoverished ones (גֶּבֶר רָשׁ וְעֹשֵׁק דַּלִּים) [is like] a sweeping rain leaving no food.' The difference between the poverty of the oppressed and that of the oppressor here will now be obvious.

Two passages in Proverbs seem to display the combined influence of the main elements connoted by this term. 'A poor man [pinched for food] (רָשׁ) is hated even by his neighbour, but a rich man's friends are many' (14 : 20) ; 'All the brethren of a poor man [food-pinched] hate him,—how much more do his neighbours go far from him !' (19 : 7). Such remarks reveal to us, in רָשׁ, one who can hold his own against another, yet with difficulty finds a bare subsistence, so that those around have nothing to expect from him ; what could he spare ?

For exercise in distinguishing between the various terms signifying 'poor,' attention may be called to Ps. 82 : 3, 4, and especially Prov. 28 : 3, 6, 8, 11, 15, 20.

14. Verbs signifying to pour out.

a. נָבַע, הַבִּיעַ.   *b.* נָתַךְ.   *c.* נָסַךְ.

d. יָצַק.   *e.* שָׁפַךְ.

a. The distinguishing idea associated with the verb נָבַע —found only once (Prov. 18 : 4) in the Qal, all other occurrences showing the Hiphil—is that of pouring forth *in a continuous stream*, as from a spring or fountain; its application is almost entirely metaphorical. One of the Proverbs (18 : 4) tells us, 'The words of a man's mouth [are like] deep waters; the fountain of wisdom [is] a pouring torrent' (נַחַל נֹבֵעַ[1]). After calling on talkative fools[1] and scorners to turn at her reproof, wisdom promises, 'I will pour out (אַבִּיעָה) my spirit unto you;' and the Hebrew sage (in Prov. 15 : 2) has observed that 'the tongue of wise men makes good use of knowledge, but the mouth of fools (כְּסִילִים[1]) pours forth (יַבִּיעַ) folly.' The verb is chiefly applied in this figurative manner to the pouring forth of words, and presents itself thus in several passages throughout the Psalms, as 119 : 171, 'My lips shall pour forth (תַּבַּעְנָה) praise when thou teachest me thy statutes;' 145 : 7, 'They shall pour forth the memory of the abundance of thy goodness;' 19 : 2, 'Day unto day poureth forth speech;' see also 78 : 2; 59 : 8; Eccl. 10 : 1.

b. The more prominent features in the meaning of the verb נָתַךְ seem to be (*a*) that the pouring is not limited in amount (cf. יָצַק), or comparatively restricted as to space (cf. שָׁפַךְ), or even narrowed into a single stream, but *copious and widely diffused*; (β) with this notion is further associated that of *great force*, which may bring disaster or distress; while (γ) the direction is downwards.

---
[1] See the remarks already made at page 29 ff.

VERBS SIGNIFYING TO POUR OUT.

A simple illustration is found in Ex. 9 : 33, where it is recorded that after the plague of thunder and hail had brought destruction on man and beast and herb in Egypt, Moses 'spread out his hands to Jehovah, and the thunders and the hail ceased, while no rain was poured down (מָטָר לֹא נִתַּךְ) upon the earth.' Again, in 2 Samuel 21 : 10, we read that Rizpah, impelled by motherly devotion, watched day and night, from the beginning till the end of harvest, over the bodies of her sons, 'until water poured down (נִתַּךְ) upon them from the heavens.' In both of these cases, the rain was obviously heavy as well as wide-spread.

We are thus enabled to feel the peculiar force of the figurative language employed to show that the displeasure of the Lord was not merely intense but directed against a multitude. In Jer. 7: 20, apostasy of the entire kingdom of Judah—the inhabitants of other cities as well as Jerusalem—draws forth these words from the Lord 'Behold, mine anger and my fury is poured out (נִתֶּכֶת) upon this place,—upon man and upon beast, and upon the trees of the field and upon the face of the ground;' while a later passage (44 : 6) presents the retrospect, 'My fury and mine anger was poured out, and consumed the cities of Judah and the streets of Jerusalem, and they became a waste and a desolation.' Similarly full and disastrous outpouring of divine displeasure is indicated in 42 : 18, where we read the words, 'As mine anger and my wrath was poured out (נִתַּךְ) upon the inhabitants of Jerusalem, so shall my wrath be poured out (תִּתַּךְ) upon you when ye enter into Egypt, and ye shall become an execration and an astonishment, and a scorn;' while the prayer of Daniel (9 : 11) affords another illustration, 'All Israel have transgressed thy law and turned aside, by not obeying thy voice; therefore hath the curse been poured out upon us' (וַתִּתַּךְ עָלֵינוּ הָאָלָה); see also ver. 27; 2 Chr. 12 : 7; 34 : 21, 25. The idea of abundant outpouring in association with distress is likewise preserved in the language of Job (3 : 24), 'Like[1] my meat cometh my sighing, and my groanings are poured out copiously (וַיִּתְּכוּ) like water;' see further 10 : 10.

We can now readily understand how naturally and appropriately this term was utilised in speaking of large masses of metal when

---

[1] For confirmation of this meaning of לִפְנֵי, see Job 4 : 19; 1 Sam. 1 : 16.

being poured out (2 Kings 22 : 9 ; 2 Chron. 34 : 17) ; the prophecies of Ezekiel (22 : 18-22) contain a passage in which this usage of the word, in relation to casting, finds forcible illustration.

c. Full consideration of all the passages in which נָסַךְ and its derivatives are employed seem to show that this verb normally signifies (a) to pour out steadily and regularly, without any special force, (β) a *limited quantity* of liquid, over (γ) an uneven but comparatively *restricted surface*, so that (δ) merely a thin but somewhat *uniform coating* is spread over the object upon which the pouring is made. These several elements constituting the whole meaning of the word are not, however, always equally obvious in every instance.

The directions regarding the drink-offering (נֶסֶךְ, or נֵסֶךְ) or libation which formed an accompaniment of certain Levitical sacrifices after the settlement of the Israelites in Canaan (Lev. 23 : 10, 13)— for it could not possibly be offered in the wilderness—afford some data useful for our purpose. With a lamb or with a kid, the drink-offering was fixed at a quarter of a hin of wine ; for a ram, the third of a hin of wine was the amount prescribed ; for a bullock, half a hin was required (Numb. 15 : 5, 7, 10 ; compare also 28 : 7, 14). These drink-offerings were not, like the blood of the slain victims, to be tossed out (זָרַק ; see Lev. 1 : 11 ; 8 : 19) against the sides of the altar, or poured out (שָׁפַךְ,[1] 4 : 18, 25, 30, 34, but יָצַק[1] in 8 : 15 ; 9 : 9) at its base ; they were poured upon (or over) the flesh of the sacrifice as it lay on the altar (Ex. 30 : 9 ; Num. 15 : 5). Moreover, the amount of liquid was varied in accordance with the size of the victim, evidently that in each case there might be sufficient to moisten the accessible *surface* of the sacrifice; and it is important in this connection to observe that, with a single exception,[2] the verb employed to signify the pouring out of the נֶסֶךְ is always the cognate נָסַךְ (but more frequently הִסִּיךְ). Thus, Exod. 30 : 9, ' A drink-offering shall ye not pour out (נֶסֶךְ לֹא תִסְּכוּ) upon it ' [viz. the altar of incense] ; Num. 28 : 7, ' Pour out a libation of strong drink (הַסֵּךְ נֶסֶךְ שֵׁכָר) to Jehovah ;' while Jeremiah repeatedly (7 : 18 ; 19 : 13 ; 32 : 29 ; 44 : 17, 18, 19, 25) declares the displeasure of the Lord against idolatrous Judah and Jerusalem in continuing to burn incense and to ' pour out

---

[1] On the difference in meaning between these terms, see below.
[2] Viz. Is. 57 : 6, a passage to be considered afterwards.

VERBS SIGNIFYING TO POUR OUT. 95

drink-offerings (הַסֵּךְ נְסָכִים) to other gods.' See also Ezek. 20 : 28 ; Ps. 16 : 4 etc. ; cf. Hos. 9 : 4.

What has just been stated enables us to determine the proper meaning of the cognate nouns נֶסֶךְ and מַסֵּכָה, when applied to an idol—the former term being thus used in Exod. 32 : 4, 8 ; 34 : 17 ; Levit. 19 : 4 ; Num. 33 : 52 ; Deut. 9 : 12, 16, etc., and the latter in Is. 41 : 29 ; 48 : 5 ; Jer. 10 : 14 ; 51 : 17. Though commonly regarded as signifying a 'molten image,' the terms cannot fairly be viewed as meaning an image of solid metal ; all the evidence rather goes to show that the words denote an idol primarily formed of wood (Isa. 30 : 22 ; 44 : 15, 17 ; 45 : 20), stone, or other suitable material, carved or graven into some definite shape (hence called פֶּסֶל), but afterwards overlaid or covered with a coating or shell of metal,—usually silver or gold. Only after this metal casing had been placed on it could the designation מַסֵּכָה (or נֶסֶךְ) be applicable to such an object; פֶּסֶל, however, might then be equally employed, yet the use of the one term rather than the other would obviously indicate the particular aspect in which the image was regarded by the speaker.

Attentive perusal of the verses in Exodus (32 : 1-8, 20 ; cf. Deut. 9 : 12, 16, 21) describing the formation and fate of the idol-calf at Horeb will afford some guidance in our search. We read (Exodus 32 : 3) that 'all the people broke off the rings of gold which were in their ears, and brought [them] to Aaron. And he took [them] from their hand, and fashioned it with a graving-tool, and[1] made it a calf, a metal-cased image' (עֵגֶל מַסֵּכָה). That these closing words must be rendered thus, or in some similar manner—for the idol was not of solid gold—becomes apparent when we read, in ver. 20, that after Moses had descended from the mount in wrath, 'he took the calf which they had made, and burned [it] (וַיִּשְׂרֹף) in the fire, and ground [it] till it became small [like dust], and strewed it upon the surface of the water, and made the children of Israel drink it.' If the idol had been wholly of metal, it could not have been said that Moses 'burned' it. The burning, accordingly, implies that the main portion of the idol must have consisted of wood, which, as we know from other passages (Isaiah 40 : 20 ; 44 : 15, 19 ; 45 : 20 ; see also Deut. 7 : 5, 25 ; 12 : 3), was most commonly used to make an idola-

---

[1] To translate וַיַּעֲשֵׂהוּ 'after he had made it...' (A. V.) is both unwarranted and misleading.

trous image. Moreover, what could the people have been 'made to drink' with the water, except the burnt wood pounded to fine ashes, which, from their less specific gravity, would float? But particles of gold would sink.

Confirmatory evidence in favour of this view is afforded by the prohibition addressed to the Israelites in Deut. 7 : 25, 'The graven images of their gods (פְּסִילֵי אֱלֹהֵיהֶם) ye shall burn with fire; thou shalt not covet any silver or gold upon them,' and particularly in Is. 30 : 22, 'Ye shall defile the [metal] covering of thy graven images of silver (צִפּוּי פְּסִילֵי כַסְפֶּךָ), and the plating of thy gold-cased image' (אֲפֻדַּת מַסֵּכַת זְהָבֶךָ). As מַסֵּכָה, in all these passages, evidently denotes a carved image covered with a plating of gold, we seem warranted in attaching the same meaning to the term when elsewhere found in like connection.

But these results likewise establish for us the correct meaning of the verb נָסַךְ in some passages which otherwise might be misunderstood. The first of these is Isaiah 40 : 19, 'The carved idol doth an artificer overlay (הַפֶּסֶל נָסַךְ חָרָשׁ), and a refiner plateth it thinly with gold' (צֹרֵף בַּזָּהָב יְרַקְּעֶנּוּ). The second passage is Isa. 44 : 10, 'Who hath fashioned a god (מִי יָצַר אֵל), or overlaid a graven image [with metal plating] (פֶּסֶל נָסָךְ)?' In neither of these two instances may we think of anything more than a small quantity of metal, and this made to form the thin casing of a carved figure.[1]

The metaphorical use of the verb in Isaiah 29 : 10 claims regard as affording a clue to further solutions. 'Jehovah hath poured out (נָסַךְ) upon you a spirit of deep sleep ([2] רוּחַ תַּרְדֵּמָה), and hath firmly closed your eyes; the prophets, and your rulers, the seers, hath he covered' (כִּפָּה). Here, נָסַךְ evidently conveys mainly the notion of completeness—not of superabundance [3]—in the outpouring; enough of heavy sleep to cause complete unconsciousness in every one was all that God's design required.

Another step enables us to find a simpler rendering of Isa. 25 : 7

---

[1] As will be shown presently, יָצַק would have been the term employed, had the idea meant to be conveyed been that of 'founding' or 'casting' into one solid mass.

[2] See the remarks already made at page 28.

[3] It will be seen afterwards that שָׁפַךְ would have been used, if this meaning had been intended.

VERBS SIGNIFYING TO POUR OUT.

than has been commonly received; there it is said that Jehovah will annihilate the wrapping which is wrapped over all the peoples, 'and the [thin but complete] covering which is spread (הַמַּסֵּכָה הַנְּסוּכָה) over all the nations.' There is no good reason for rendering these words 'the thick veil (or 'web') that is woven.'

d. The pouring indicated by יָצַק may be described in the main as neither copious nor violent nor diffused, but rather as (α) limited in amount, (β) steady and gentle as to manner, (γ) concentrated as regards place, and (δ) frequently directed into—not always upon—its object. These several elements of the general meaning are not however, equally perceptible in every case.

The pouring out of oil[1] illustrates these remarks. At Aaron's consecration to the priesthood, Moses received commandment from the Lord (Exodus 29 : 7), 'Thou shalt take the oil of anointing and shalt pour (וְיָצַקְתָּ) [it] upon his head.' In anointing Saul as king (1 Sam. 10 : 1), Samuel 'took the flask of oil (פַּךְ הַשֶּׁמֶן) and poured (וַיִּצֹק) [it] upon his head' (cf. Lev. 8 : 12 ; 21 : 10). Elisha, in commissioning one of the sons of the prophets to anoint Jehu as king over Israel, says, 'Take the flask of oil and pour (וְיָצַקְתָּ) [it] upon his head.' On inanimate objects also, oil was similarly poured to indicate consecration for divine service ; thus, when Jacob arose after his memorable vision at Bethel (Gen. 28 : 18), he set up his stone pillow as a sacred pillar, 'and poured out (וַיִּצֹק) oil upon the top of it;' and it was ordained (Levit. 2 : 1, 6) that oil was always to be poured out upon the sacrificial meal-offering of fine flour. In all such instances, the quantity of liquid used was small, while the pouring was quiet and steady, and directed upon the person or thing thereby consecrated ; but similar remarks apply to the common operation mentioned in 2 Kings 3 : 11, where Elisha is introduced as the one who 'poured water (יָצַק מַיִם) on the hands of Elijah.' Consider also the limitation evident in 1 Kings 18 : 33, where we find Elijah's command at Carmel regarding the sacrifice to Jehovah, 'Fill ye four jars[2] (כַּדִּים) with water, and pour (וְיִצְקוּ) [it] upon the burnt-offering and upon the pieces of wood.'

---

[1] Viz. שֶׁמֶן ; see the explanation already given at page 49 ff.
[2] Not 'barrels,' as in the Authorised and the Revised Versions ; see what is stated below.

The conclusions we have already reached enable us to appreciate the exact force of the words employed in the original text of Genesis 35 : 14. After Jacob's second vision at Bethel, on his return from Paddan-aram, he set up a stone pillar, 'and poured a drink-offering (וַיַּסֵּךְ נֶסֶךְ) over it, and poured out oil (וַיִּצֹק שֶׁמֶן) upon it.' The different kinds of pouring will be obvious.

But the pouring signified by יָצַק might also be directed *into* an object. So, the priest who re-admitted a cured leper into the community had to pour into the hollow of his left hand some of the oil brought by the offerer, and to sprinkle it as the law enjoined (Lev. 14 : 15, 26). The impoverished widow relieved by Elisha poured out from her small bottle of oil, miraculously multiplied, into the vessels borrowed from her neighbours, till there was abundance to provide means for paying her debts (2 Kings 4 : 4, 5). Later, the same prophet, after freeing the poisoned pottage from its deadly power, commanded the attendant, 'Pour out to the people (צַק לָעָם) that they may eat ; and there was no harm in the pot' (ver. 38-41). And one of Ezekiel's messages contains the command (24 : 3), 'Set on the caldron, and also pour water into it' (יְצֹק בּוֹ מָיִם). Consider further the brief but beautiful line in Ps. 45 : 3, 'Grace is poured into thy lips' (הוּצַק חֵן בְּשִׂפְתוֹתֶיךָ).

The application of יָצַק to signify the pouring out of molten metal is an easy step further, and here the appropriate English rendering of the verb is to 'cast,' or 'found.' As might be expected, we find the term introduced in such passages in Exodus as treat of the articles, formed of solid metal, which were required in the construction of the Tabernacle. Among the directions given to Moses concerning the preparation of the ark, we find these words (25 : 11, 12), 'Thou shalt overlay it with pure gold...and thou shalt cast (וְיָצַקְתָּ) for it four rings of gold, and put them upon the four feet thereof' (cf. 37 : 3, 13). Similarly, we read that Bezaleel overlaid the altar of burnt-offering with copper, 'and cast (וַיִּצֹק) four rings' for attachment to the sides. Copper sockets were cast for some of the pillars (Ex. 26 : 37), and silver sockets for others (36 : 36 ; cf. 38 : 27). In the construction of Solomon's Temple, also, even more numerous castings were required (see 1 Kings 7 : 16, 23, 24, 30, 33); every one of these, however, distinctly exemplifies the special peculiarities in the meaning of יָצַק, as an outpouring which is essentially regular

VERBS SIGNIFYING TO POUR OUT.

and steady, confined in the direction of its course, and restricted as to quantity.[1]

But the *result* of fusing and casting metal presents a fresh idea associated with יָצַק, viz. that of firmness or fixity; this development of meaning is principally illustrated in the Book of Job. Thus, in 41:15, it is said of leviathan, 'The folds of his flesh cleave closely together; [each one is] firm (יָצוּק) upon him, it cannot be moved. His heart is firm (יָצוּק) as a stone, and firm (יָצוּק) as a nether millstone.' See also Ps. 41:9.

In Job 22:15, this developed meaning seems the only one that is at all appropriate. The whole passage, as it stands, is confessedly difficult; but such translations of the closing words נָהָר יוּצַק יְסוֹדָם as, 'whose foundation was overflown with a flood,' or 'whose foundation was poured out as a stream,' or 'their foundation is like an overflowing river,' hardly suit the context. Moreover, as we have already seen, יָצַק is never applied to a 'flood,' or a full 'stream,' or 'river.' But by a very slight emendation of the Masoretic text, so that we may read כָּהָר instead of נָהָר, and by attaching to יָצַק the later idea of firmness so clearly marked elsewhere in Job, the clause may more appropriately be rendered, 'though their foundation be firm [or 'established'] like a mountain.'[2]

In some other passages, however, it would seem better to suppose that, through similarity of sound, a form of יָצַק has been substituted for another from יָצַג, than attribute to the former root a rather unusual sense. In 2 Sam. 15:24, it is recorded that among those who were leaving Jerusalem with David, in his flight from Absalom, were the Levites who bore the ark of the covenant, 'and they set down' the ark of God; instead of וַיַּצִּקוּ, it seems preferable to read וַיַּצִּגוּ.[3] In Josh. 7:23, we read that the messengers sent to Achan's

---

[1] Here also may be cited an expression found in the address of Elihu to Job (37:18), where the sky is said to be 'like a molten mirror' (כִּרְאִי מוּצָק). Such a reflecting instrument, be it remembered, used to be made of metal cast so as to present a smooth surface, which was afterwards highly polished.

[2] That a narrowly written כ might easily be mistaken for נ is obvious. In 2 Kings 14:10, we find הַכֵּה הִכִּיתָ, whereas the parallel passage, 2 Chr. 25:19 gives הִנֵּה הִכִּיתָ. Again, in Micah 1:10, by his rendering, μὴ οἰκοδομεῖτε, the Septuagint translator shows that he read אַל־תִּבְנוּ instead of אַל־תִּבְכּוּ.

[3] As suggested by Driver, Budde, and others; the rendering of the Septuagint (ἔστησαν) supports this view.

tent brought back the stolen goods 'and placed them' before the Lord ; here, similarly, for וַיַצִּקֵם, we ought to read וַיַצִּגֵם. Possibly also, after slight alterations of the Masoretic text,[1] we might thus interpret Job 11 : 15, 'Then verily thou shalt lift up thy face without tottering, and thou shalt be established without fear.'

Remarks on Lev. 8 : 15 ; 9 : 9, and 1 Kings 22 : 35 are deferred till a later stage in our investigations.

e. The verb שָׁפַךְ signifies to pour out, not diffusively, but (α) at one spot, where the discharge is (β) large and (γ) forceful. Further, (δ) the contents are for the most part liquid, but the verb is sometimes used with reference to dust or stones, and (figuratively) to wrath, etc.

The frequently recurring phrase 'to shed blood' (שָׁפַךְ דָּם) illustrates these remarks. Every one knows that this expression signifies the rapid, violent, and complete outpouring of life's liquid at one spot. Earliest in the Scripture record stands the legal prescription (Gen. 9 : 6), 'Whoso sheddeth man's blood, by man shall his blood be shed' (שֹׁפֵךְ דַּם הָאָדָם), but concrete instances are also numerous. Dissuading his more cruel-hearted brethren from their wicked purpose towards Joseph, Reuben says (Gen. 37 : 21, 22) 'Let us not kill him ; do not shed any blood (אַל־תִּשְׁפְּכוּ־דָם) ; cast him into this pit.' Joab's murder of the unsuspecting Abner (2 Sam. 3 : 27), and his treacherous assassination of Amasa (2 Sam. 20 : 10), are referred to afterwards by Solomon (1 Kings 2 : 31) as 'blood which Joab shed causelessly' (דְּמֵי חִנָּם אֲשֶׁר שָׁפַךְ יוֹאָב). Manasseh's name is lastingly disgraced, not merely by his idol-worship, but by foul murders of his subjects ; for 'very much innocent blood did Manasseh shed (דָּם נָקִי שָׁפַךְ מְנַשֶּׁה הַרְבֵּה מְאֹד), until he filled Jerusalem from one end to another' (2 Kings 21 : 16). David's proposal to build the Temple was declined on the ground that he had shed much blood (1 Chron. 22 : 8 ; 28 : 3). See also Deut. 21 : 7 ; Psalm 79 : 3, 10 ; 106 : 38 ; Prov. 1 : 16 ; 6 : 17 ; Jerem. 7 : 6 ; 22 : 3 ; Ezek. 18 : 10 ; 23 : 8, 45, etc.

Similarly, when this expression (שָׁפַךְ דָּם) is used with reference to the lower animals—whether slaughtered for consumption of their

---

[1] Substitute מָמוֹט for the Masoretic מָמוּם, and then read וְהָיִיתָ מֻצָּג instead of וְהָיִיתָ מֻצָּק.

flesh as ordinary food, or killed for sacrifice—the same ideas must be held as meant to be conveyed. In Deut. 12:15, 16, explicit directions are laid down for the preparation, at a distance from the sanctuary and the appointed altar there, of the flesh of clean animals that might be eaten: 'only, ye shall not eat the blood; upon the earth shall ye pour it out (תִּשְׁפְּכֶנּוּ) like water;' see also ver. 24, and 15:23. The blood was to be poured out quickly, completely, and collectively. In those passages also which give direction regarding the disposal of the mass of the blood drawn from sacrificial victims—for some was always put at least upon the horns of the altar, if not elsewhere also—it was ever required that the sacrificing priest should 'pour out all the blood at the bottom of the altar,' Exodus 29:12; Lev. 4:7, 18, 25, 30, 34. In all these instances, the expression employed is שָׁפַךְ דָּם, and we now know how the phrase is to be understood.

Specially noteworthy and instructive are passages which mention outpouring of indignation, or fury, or wrath. Bold strokes in the picture of Jerusalem's desolation, displayed in the Book of Lamentations, are those which reveal the mind of the Lord: 'He hath poured out his fury like fire (שָׁפַךְ כָּאֵשׁ חֲמָתוֹ); the Lord was like an enemy' (2:4, 5); 'The Lord hath spent his fury; he hath poured out the heat of his anger (שָׁפַךְ חֲרוֹן אַפּוֹ), and hath kindled a fire in Zion' (4:11). The discharge is fierce and full and forceful, and concentrated upon one point,—Jerusalem. Language of kindred character is chosen in Ezekiel's prophecies to indicate the fierce displeasure of the Lord, and the discriminate determination of that wrath upon its proper object: 'I will pour out [abundantly] my fury (לִשְׁפֹּךְ חֲמָתִי) upon them; I will spend mine anger (לְכַלּוֹת אַפִּי) upon them' (20:8; cf. verses 13, 21; so also 21:36); 'with fury poured out (בְּחֵמָה שְׁפוּכָה) will I rule over you' (20:33; cf. ver. 28). Consider also the prayer in Ps. 69:25, directed against the enemies of the Lord's righteous servant, 'Pour out upon them thine indignation' (שְׁפָךְ־עֲלֵיהֶם זַעְמֶךָ); and again, the language of Psalm 79:6, against those who desecrated and destroyed the Temple, 'Pour out thy wrath against the nations' (שְׁפֹךְ חֲמָתְךָ אֶל־הַגּוֹיִם). Fulness of outpouring and well concentrated energy are distinctly evident in all these passages.

Most of the same features are visible even when שָׁפַךְ is applied to the pouring out of dust, stones, earth, or ashes. In the Mosaic law regarding leprosy, when this had been discovered in the walls of a house, it was required (Lev. 14 : 41) that the priest should 'cause the house to be scraped within, round about, and that they should pour out the dust[1] (וְשָׁפְכוּ אֶת־הֶעָפָר) which they had scraped off, outside of the city, into an unclean place.' A prominent feature here —the pouring out of the whole at one spot, into a single heap—is more frequently presented in those passages which refer to mounds of earth raised outside a city by besiegers. Jeremiah thus warns Jerusalem of national disaster coming from the north (6 : 6), 'Cut down trees, and raise a siege-mound (שִׁפְכוּ סֹלְלָה) against Jerusalem;' while Ezekiel (26 : 8), predicting Nebuchadnezzar's advance against Tyre, declares, 'Thy daughters in the field shall he slay with the sword, and he shall make a fort against thee, and raise against thee a siege-mound' (וְשָׁפַךְ עָלַיִךְ סֹלְלָה); see further 17 : 17; 21 : 27; 2 Sam. 20 : 15; 2 Kings 19 : 32 (or Is. 37 : 33); Dan. 11 : 15.

The results now obtained enable us to read, with greater confidence regarding their true meaning, certain passages in which the use of terms is to be noted carefully.

Let us first consider Lev. 8 : 15 and 9 : 9. In the former of these two passages, we read that when Moses consecrated Aaron and his sons to the priesthood, he put upon the horns of the altar some of the blood from the bullock slain as a sin-offering, but the remainder of 'the blood he poured out (אֶת־הַדָּם יָצַק) at the base of the altar.' Similarly, in the latter passage, which records the offering, eight days afterwards, of the first expiatory sacrifice presented by Aaron for himself as installed priest, we read that after putting some of the blood from the calf upon the horns of the altar, the rest of 'the blood he poured out (אֶת־הַדָּם יָצַק) at the base of the altar.' The fact that in these two verses alone is יָצַק employed to indicate the pouring out of the mass of the blood at the foot of the altar, while שָׁפַךְ is the term introduced everywhere else under similar circumstances, seems at least to mark that the outpouring—for whatever reason—was steadily and gently performed.

In Is. 57 : 6, the Lord thus complains against apostate Israel for their worship of idols : 'to them also thou hast poured out a drink-

---

[1] See the subsequent discussion on words signifying 'dust.'

VERBS SIGNIFYING TO POUR OUT.   103

offering (שָׁפַכְתָּ נֶסֶךְ), thou hast offered a meal-offering.' Only here in all Scripture is שָׁפַךְ used with reference to the pouring out of a drink-offering, נָסַךְ (or הִפִּיךְ) being found everywhere else. Is this unique selection meant to mark the eager lavishness of the idolaters in worshipping their gods?

Comparison of 1 Kings 18 : 28 with 22 : 35 enables us to read both passages with keener interest and more exact appreciation of their saddening details. In the former, the sacred historian relates that the prophets of Baal at Carmel, maddened by disappointment, cut themselves with swords and lances till they 'made [1] blood gush out upon themselves' (עַד־שְׁפָךְ־דָּם עֲלֵיהֶם). On the other hand, in the account of Ahab's end, we see him wounded, carried from the field of battle, yet 'supported in the chariot (וְהַמֶּלֶךְ הָיָה מָעֳמָד בַּמֶּרְכָּבָה), and the blood from the wound oozed [2] slowly out' (וַיִּצֶק דַּם־הַמַּכָּה). Thus Ahab slowly bled to death.

Lastly, let us compare the difference of language in some gracious promises of God. Is. 44 : 3 runs thus : 'I will pour water (אֶצָק־מַיִם) upon one who is thirsty, and streams upon dry ground ; I will pour out (אֶצֹק) my spirit upon thy seed, and my blessing upon thine offspring.' The selection of יָצַק would seem to indicate that, in this outpouring, with steadiness and gentleness there was combined restriction, limitation in bestowal,—that sufficiency was to be granted, but not superfluity.

But let us note the contrast with some other promises, and first, one of abundant consolation through Ezekiel (39 : 29) to the exiled Hebrews, 'I will no more hide [3] (לֹא־אַסְתִּיר עוֹד) my face from them, for I have poured out my spirit (שָׁפַכְתִּי אֶת־רוּחִי) upon the house of Israel, declareth the Lord God.' Next let us consider the utterance in Zech. 12 : 9, 10, 'I will seek to destroy all the nations that come against Jerusalem ; and I will pour out (וְשָׁפַכְתִּי) upon the house of David and upon the inhabitants of Jerusalem the spirit of grace and supplication, and they shall look upon him whom they have pierced, and they shall mourn for him as one mourneth for his only son, and be in bitterness for him as one is in bitterness for his first-born.'

---

[1] The verb is always transitive ; hence the clause should not be rendered, as in several Versions, 'until blood gushed out upon them.'

[2] Obviously, 'ran' is too strong a rendering.

[3] See the explanation already given at page 71 ff.

Finally, let us mark the terms of the promise in Joel 3 : 1, 2, 'I will pour out my spirit (אֶשְׁפּוֹךְ אֶת־רוּחִי) upon all flesh, and your sons and your daughters shall prophesy, your old men shall dream dreams, your young men shall see visions, and also upon the servants and upon the handmaidens in those days will I pour out (אֶשְׁפּוֹךְ) my spirit.' Does not the fact that שָׁפַךְ (not יָצַק) is used in these three passages, lead us to think of special liberality and heartiness?

15. Nouns signifying Rain.

a. מָטָר,　b. גֶּשֶׁם,　c. זֶרֶם,　d. מוֹרֶה, יוֹרֶה,　e. מַלְקוֹשׁ,
f. רְבִיבִים,　g. שְׂעִירִים,　h. סַגְרִיר,　i. זַרְזִיף.

Rain falls very regularly in Palestine at expected seasons, beginning gradually about the end of October with the 'former rain,' and continuing somewhat steadily during the winter; the heaviest fall is experienced during November and December. After the month of March—the season of the 'latter rain'—showers become lighter and less frequent, and about the opening of May, they nearly altogether cease. No rain descends in June, July, August, and September, excepting on occasions so phenomenal as to excite astonishment and fear.[1] Allusion to the rarity of such events is made in Prov. 26 : 1, 'As snow in summer and rain in harvest, so honour is not seemly for a fool' ([2] כְּסִיל); while every one will readily recall the miracle performed in answer to the prayer of Samuel (1 Sam. 12 : 17, 18), 'Is it not wheat harvest to-day? I will call unto the Lord that he may send thunder and rain, and ye shall know and see that your wickedness is great which ye have done in the sight of the Lord, in asking a king for yourselves. So Samuel called unto the Lord, and the Lord sent thunder and rain that day, and all the people greatly feared the Lord and Samuel.'

a. Of all the words signifying *rain*, מָטָר is the most frequently employed. It is a generic noun, comprehending other more specific

---

[1] As the physical conformation of Palestine presents considerable variety of elevation, these remarks regarding climate are but general; there is obviously a great difference between Lebanon and the depressed valley of the Jordan.

[2] See previous remarks regarding this term, page 29.

terms, as seen in the divine promise, 'I will give the rain of your land (מְטַר אַרְצְכֶם) in its season,—the former rain and the latter rain (יוֹרֶה וּמַלְקוֹשׁ), that thou mayest gather in thy grain and thy vine-crop and thine olive-crop'[2] (Deut. 11 : 14). This passage likewise affords an excellent illustration of the fact that מָטָר specially means a copious yet not quite a 'heavy' rain; in other words, it is usually applied to rain regarded as a *beneficial* (rather than an injurious[3]) natural agent, refreshing and fertilising the soil. Another instructive promise is given in Deut. 28 : 12, 'The Lord shall open unto thee his good treasure, the heaven to give the rain of thy land (מְטַר אַרְצְךָ) in its season;' see also Ps. 147 : 8; Job 5 : 10. On the other hand, the withholding of this abundant rain meant the denial of all those heavenly gifts which are the fruits of the soil; concerning his vineyard, the house of Israel, the Lord declared through Isaiah (5 : 6), 'I will also command the clouds not to rain any rain (מֵהַמְטִיר מָטָר) upon it;' and the nation was solemnly warned against idolatry, lest the Lord should 'shut up the heaven, so that there be no rain, and that the soil yield not its produce' (Deut. 11 : 17). See also 2 Sam. 1 : 21; 1 Kings 18 : 1.

So foreign to מָטָר, in itself, is the notion of damage, that it is not applied to an injurious rain unless a qualifying adjective be added, to express this distinctly, as in Prov. 28 : 3, 'A strong man in want [of food], and forcibly defrauding impoverished ones, [is like] sweeping rain (מָטָר סֹחֵף) leaving no food.'[4] Cf. Is. 4 : 6.

b. That גֶּשֶׁם denotes a heavy, *drenching rain*, descending from a sky darkened with clouds, and generally accompanied with violent wind, is tolerably evident even from the proverb '[Like] clouds and wind, but no pouring rain at all (גֶּשֶׁם אָיִן), is a man who boasts of a deceptive gift' (25 : 14). Further proof is given in Elijah's words to Ahab at Carmel (1 Kings 18 : 41), 'Get thee up, eat and drink, for there is the sound of abundance of soaking rain' (קוֹל הֲמוֹן הַגֶּשֶׁם), and his later message to the king (ver. 44), 'Yoke [thy chariot] and go down, that the drenching rain (הַגֶּשֶׁם) may not stop thee. And it came to pass in a little, after the heavens had become black with clouds and wind, that there was a great drenching rain (גֶּשֶׁם גָּדוֹל),

---

[1] These terms will be more fully explained below.   [2] See page 47.
[3] Contrast the meaning associated with זֶרֶם.   [4] See also page 91.

NOUNS SIGNIFYING RAIN.

and Ahab rode and went to Jezreel.' Allusion to the darkness and storm which precede and accompany this heavy rain is likewise made in the prophecy of Elisha before Jehoram and Jehoshaphat (2 Kings 3 : 17), 'Ye shall not see wind, neither shall ye see heavy rain (גֶּשֶׁם), yet shall that valley be filled with water.' Reference is made in the Book of Ezra (10 : 13) to the discomfort felt by human beings exposed to such heavy rains; the congregation pleaded for consideration, even while acknowledging their sins; 'As thou hast said, so will we do. Nevertheless, the people are numerous, and the season [is that of] heavy rains (הָעֵת גְּשָׁמִים), and we have no strength to stand without' (cf. also v. 9).[1] It may be sufficient to add that this same term is very properly employed to designate the heavy rain that fell upon the earth during the Deluge (הַמַּבּוּל [2]). We read in Gen. 7 : 12, that 'the heavy rain (גֶּשֶׁם) was upon the earth for forty days and forty nights,' and afterwards (Gen. 8 : 2), when enough had been poured out, that then 'the heavy rain from heaven (הַגֶּשֶׁם מִן־הַשָּׁמַיִם) was restrained.'

Though the word is thus applied to a heavy and even a violent down-pour from the heavens, it does not usually mean such rain as brings destruction or ruin; it is rather (like מָטָר) a refreshing and fertilising rain. This is evidenced by the terms of Jehovah's promise recorded in Ezekiel 34 : 26, 'I will bring down the heavy rain in its season (הַגֶּשֶׁם בְּעִתּוֹ); heavy rains of blessing (גִּשְׁמֵי בְרָכָה) shall there be;' and again by the similar promise made in Levit. 26 : 4, 'I will give your heavy rains in their season (גִשְׁמֵיכֶם בְּעִתָּם), so that the earth shall give her increase, and the tree of the field shall give its fruit;' while the withholding of such a blessing is, in Zech. 14 : 17, threatened as a punishment in return for withholding honour from God; 'Whosoever will not come up, from the families of the earth, to Jerusalem, to worship the King, Jehovah of hosts,—upon them there shall not be the abundant rain' (גֶּשֶׁם); see also Jer. 14 : 4. That גֶּשֶׁם signifies heavy rain as a refresher and fertiliser of the soil is further shown by its occasional use as a general term—just like מָטָר [2]—including the more specific 'former rain' and 'latter rain.' The best illustrations are found in Jer. 5 : 24, 'Let us fear Jehovah

---

[1] The date is given in ver. 9 as the twentieth day of the ninth month (Chisleu), which corresponds to our December, and forms part of the season during which the 'former rain' falls. [2] See above, page 105.

our God, who giveth [heavy] rain—the former rain and latter rain—in its season' (הֹתֵן הַגֶּשֶׁם יוֹרֶה וּמַלְקוֹשׁ בְּעִתּוֹ), who preserveth for us appointed weeks of harvest;' and in Joel 2 : 23, 'He bringeth down for you rain—former rain and latter rain' (גֶּשֶׁם מוֹרֶה וּמַלְקוֹשׁ).

As the גֶּשֶׁם, though a heavy and soaking rain, is not usually damaging, express mention must be made of this idea when meant to be associated with such rain. An excellent illustration is found in Ezek. 38 : 22, presenting the words of the Lord against Gog; 'an inundating heavy rain (גֶּשֶׁם שׁוֹטֵף) and hailstones, fire and brimstone, will I rain upon him;' a like example occurs in 13 : 11. Obviously, however, no specification is necessary in such a passage as Psalm 105 : 32, where the reference is to one of the ten plagues which were sent on the Egyptians, 'He gave their heavy rains [in the form of] hail' (נָתַן גִּשְׁמֵיהֶם בָּרָד).

c. By far the strongest meaning is conveyed by זֶרֶם (found only in the prophetical and poetical writings), which may frequently be rendered *rain-storm*, or even *waterspout*; it signifies an overwhelming storm of rain, swelling into an inundating flood, and sweeping every object with destructive force.[1] The general idea of a 'tempest,' however, predominates, so that the term, though often found alone, sometimes assumes a specifying genitive—as 'water,' 'hail'—to define the form assumed by the elements. The term is used alone in Isa. 30 : 30, 'The Lord shall cause the majesty of his voice to be heard......with crashing and rain-storm (זֶרֶם) and hail;' and again in 32 : 2, 'A man shall be like a [complete] covert from wind (כְּמַחֲבֵא־רוּחַ [2]), and a retreat from a rain-storm' (סֵתֶר זָרֶם [3]); and once more, in 4 : 6, 'and a booth shall be for a shade by day from heat, and for a refuge and a retreat from rain-storm and [ordinary] rain' (מִזֶּרֶם וּמִמָּטָר); see also Job 24 : 8. More frequently, however, a determining word is superadded, as in Hab. 3 : 10, 'The mount-

---

[1] Although the cognate verb occurs but twice, both passages give us further light. In Ps. 90 : 5, where the Almighty is addressed as carrying off generation after generation of mortals, the Psalmist tersely and expressively adds זְרַמְתָּם,—a word which cannot be succinctly rendered in English, but may perhaps be paraphrased, 'Thou overwhelmest them as with a rain-storm and carriest them away with its flood.' Ps. 77 : 18, where the Poel is used, may be rendered, 'The clouds poured out a storm of waters' (זֹרְמוּ מַיִם עָבוֹת).

[2] See remarks already made at page 77 ff.   [3] See page 71 ff.

NOUNS SIGNIFYING RAIN.

ains saw thee and writhed; the tempest of waters (זֶרֶם מַיִם) passed by.' But the most instructive instance is Isa. 28 : 2, 'As a storm of hail (זֶרֶם בָּרָד), a tempest of destruction, as a storm of mighty waters sweeping along ([1] כְּזֶרֶם מַיִם כַּבִּירִים שֹׁטְפִים) shall he cast down to the earth with violence.' Careful note should likewise be made of terms employed by the same prophet in a psalm of praise (25 : 4) to the Lord, 'Thou hast been a stronghold to the impoverished ([2] לַדָּל), a stronghold to the helpless poor ([3] לָאֶבְיוֹן) in his distress,—a place of refuge from a rain-storm (מִזֶּרֶם), a shade from heat; for the blast of those who are dreadful in might (עָרִיצִים) is like a rain-storm [against the side] of a wall ([4] כְּזֶרֶם קִיר).

d, e. מוֹרֶה or יוֹרֶה (each of these forms being found twice, viz. in Deut. 11 : 14, Jer. 5 : 24, and Ps. 84 : 7, Joel 2 : 23), the 'former (or early) rain,' and מַלְקוֹשׁ the 'latter rain,' are terms which rather point to the periodic character of the rains, as falling regularly at particular seasons, than indicate anything about the nature of the rainfall itself. This will be obvious from the language employed in passages already cited, in which these periodic rains are sometimes ranged under מָטָר [5], sometimes under גֶּשֶׁם.[6]

The 'early rain' begins after autumn and continues two months, —from about the middle or near the end of October, after the seed has been sown, till the middle of December. Distinct reference to its beneficial effects is made in Ps. 84 : 7, 'Passing through the valley of weeping, they make it a place of springs; with blessings also doth early rain (מוֹרֶה) cover it.'

The 'latter rain' comes at the end of the winter, falling in Palestine during March and April. How highly the husbandman valued seasonable rain, but especially this 'latter rain,' as the indispensable means of producing good crops, appears from Job 29 : 23, where the patriarch says, 'They waited for me as [for ordinary] rain (כַּמָּטָר), and their mouth they opened wide [as] for latter rain' (לְמַלְקוֹשׁ); and again, in Prov. 16 : 15, 'In the light of a king's countenance is life, and his favour is like a cloud of latter rain' (כְּעָב מַלְקוֹשׁ). Further,

---

[1] See the explanation given on page 19.   [2] See page 83.
[3] See page 81.   [4] See the remarks at page 10.
[5] See Deut. 11 : 14, already quoted on page 106.
[6] See Jer. 5 : 24 and Joel 2 : 23 (cited on the preceding page).

the prophet Hosea (6 : 3) touchingly points to the regular and invariable order of nature, in the daily rising of the sun, as an absolutely sure ground of confidence in the coming of the Lord himself; but we are also reminded, in the regular return of the rainy season, that his coming is with blessing to the world : 'Let us follow on to know the Lord ; his going forth is sure as the dawn ; and he shall come to us like the heavy rain (גֶּשֶׁם), like latter rain watering the earth (כְּמַלְקוֹשׁ יוֹרֶה אָרֶץ).' An instructive group of synonyms signifying rain is found in Joel 2 : 23, 'Rejoice ye in Jehovah your God, for he hath given you early rain (מוֹרֶה) in due measure, and sent down to you heavy rain,—early rain and latter rain' (גֶּשֶׁם מוֹרֶה וּמַלְקוֹשׁ).

f. The plural form רְבִיבִים[1] signifies light and *gentle showers*, ever welcome because they refresh and revive the thirsty ground, and never damage even tender plants. One of the best illustrations is found in Mic. 5 : 6, 'The remnant of Jacob shall be in the midst of many peoples like dew (טַל) from the presence of Jehovah, like gentle showers upon herbage' (כִּרְבִיבִים עֲלֵי־עֵשֶׂב). Ps. 65 : 11 celebrates the goodness of God in preparing the earth for the reception of seed, 'With gentle showers dost thou dissolve it' (בִּרְבִיבִים תְּמוֹגְגֶנָּה) ; while the weeping prophet (Jer. 3 : 3), lamenting the apostasy of Israel, points out how the Lord has been manifesting his displeasure, 'Gentle showers (רְבִבִים) have been withholden, and there hath been no latter rain' (מַלְקוֹשׁ) ; and later (14 : 22), the same prophet shows that Jehovah alone can send both heavy rain and gentle showers, when he asks, 'Are there [any] among the vanities [*i. e.* idols] of the Gentiles that bring down drenching rain (מַגְשִׁמִים), or can the heavens give gentle showers' (רְבִבִים) ?

g. Though שָׂעִיר is employed elsewhere in Scripture with other meanings (as 'he-goat,' etc.), the plural form שְׂעִירִים is once found, in a poetical passage—the opening of Moses' song, in Deut. 32 : 2— where it evidently signifies fine, *small rain*, 'Let my doctrine drop like abundant rain (כַּמָּטָר), let my speech flow down like the dew (כַּטַּל), like fine rain upon fresh and tender grass (כִּשְׂעִירִם עֲלֵי־דֶשֶׁא), and like gentle showers upon herbage' (כִּרְבִיבִים עֲלֵי־עֵשֶׂב). It is sig-

---

[1] The derivation (from רָבַב 'to be many') evidently points to multitudinous rain-drops.

nificant that the softer שְׂעִירִים are here associated with the tender
דֶּשֶׁא, while the heavier רְבִיבִים are introduced in connection with the
hardier עֵשֶׂב. The mass of different terms with allied meaning, all
occurring in one and the same verse, is somewhat remarkable.

h. Inferentially, and after considering the meaning of a similar
word found in Aramaic, the ἅπαξ λεγόμενον סַגְרִיר, in Prov. 27 : 15,
may be held to signify 'rain.' But this assigned force must further
be intensified, in accordance with the duplication of the third radical in the form, so as to bear the sense of *much rain*,—probably with
the additional element of discomfort which it brings.   ' A constant
dropping on a very drizzly day (בְּיוֹם סַגְרִיר), and a contentious woman, are alike.'   Some would derive the word from סָגַר ' to shut in,
enclose,' and take the expression to mean a day on which one is ob-
liged to confine himself to the house through the inclemency of the
weather, while others look to an Arabic root which signifies to 'fill
with water.'

i. A second ἅπαξ λεγόμενον, זַרְזִיף, in Psalm 72 : 6, would seem,
from its derivation [1] and the context, to signify light drops of rain
sprinkled on the earth : ' May he descend like copious rain (כְּמָטָר)
upon mown grass (גֵּז), like gentle showers scattered upon the earth '
(כִּרְבִיבִים זַרְזִיף אָרֶץ).   On any view, the form, the construction, and
the precise meaning of this word are difficult to determine.

---

[1] The biliteral element זר (cf. זָרַע, זָרַב, זָרָה, etc.) evidently presents the idea
of *scattering*.

16. Nouns signifying a Rock, Cliff, or Crag.

a. כֵּפִים.   *b.* צוּר.   *c.* סֶלַע.   *d.* שֵׁן.

a. The plural כֵּפִים (presumably from a singular form כֵּף) occurs but twice, and can evidently mean nothing but *rock-caverns*, concealed from view, and difficult of access through their height above the ordinary level of the ground, so that they are naturally fitted as hiding-places for fugitives. Thus Job (30:6) speaking strongly of the careless ones who derided him, points out that they are really social outcasts, compelled 'to dwell in holes of the ground and rock-caverns' (חֹרֵי עָפָר וְכֵפִים). Even more instructive, however, are the words of Jeremiah (4:29) in his vision of Jerusalem's coming calamity: 'At the noise of the horsemen and archers, the whole city fleeth [secretly] (בֹּרַחַת[1] כָּל־הָעִיר); they enter into the thickets and ascend[2] into the rock-caverns' (בָּאוּ בֶּעָבִים וּבַכֵּפִים עָלוּ).

b. The distinctive idea associated with צוּר—which frequently occurs in the poetic books of the Old Testament—is that of stability or solidity, as is evident in the question, 'Who is a rock (צוּר), save our God?' (Ps. 18:31; 2 Sam. 22:32), or again (Job 18:4), 'Can a rock (צוּר) be removed from its place?' A passage in Nahum (1:6), however, points rather to another feature, viz. its hardness of texture; here the prophet, to show the resistless power of God, records that 'the rocks are broken in pieces (הַצֻּרִים נִתְּצוּ) by him.' Hence this term צוּר[3] is very often applied to God as the sure foundation for the faith of his believing people: 'Trust ye in Jehovah for ever, for in Jah Jehovah is the rock of ages' (צוּר עוֹלָמִים), Is. 26:4. This thought is particularly prominent in the Psalms; thus (73:26)

---

[1] Regarding the peculiar meaning of this term, see page 3.
[2] The common rendering, 'climb up upon the rocks,' is inaccurate.
[3] But סֶלַע also is occasionally used (cf. Ps. 42:10) to express the same idea.

NOUNS SIGNIFYING A ROCK.   113

'My flesh and my heart faileth, but God is the strength [*lit.* rock] of my heart (צוּר לְבָבִי) and my portion for ever;' 'Unto thee, O Jehovah, will I cry, O my rock' (צוּרִי, 28 : 1); 'Bow down to me thine ear; deliver me speedily; be thou a strong rock (צוּר מָעוֹז), a house of defence to save me' (31 : 3).

The idea of considerable size or height is not essential to this word. We read, in Job 22 : 24, of 'pebbles of the brooks' (צוּר נְחָלִים); it is significant that the city of Tyre (צוֹר) is built upon a broad reef of rock, not on a high cliff; while the few passages in which the notion of height is presented, as Num. 23 : 9 ('From the top of the rocks I see him'), and Ps. 61 : 3 ('Lead me to the rock that is higher than I [or, too high for me']), may, after all, refer to rocks comparatively low. It is further noteworthy that we never read of such a rock affording a protecting shade, so that it presumably had sloping sides. (Contrast סֶלַע, below).

A hard and splinty texture is also implied in such an expression as 'the rock of flint' (צוּר הַחַלָּמִישׁ), Deut. 8 : 15, and especially in the command addressed to Joshua (5 : 2, 3), to make knives of stone (or flint, חַרְבוֹת צֻרִים) for circumcising the Israelites. It is always this term, and never סֶלַע, that is associated with the specific name for flint, viz. חַלָּמִישׁ.

c. The term סֶלַע properly signifies a precipitous rock,—*a cliff,* or *crag.* We shall see that the idea of exceeding height is not always very prominent.

The face of a lofty crag, obviously difficult or even impossible for man to climb, is naturally chosen as a safe habitation. Beautiful allusion to such selection is made in the bold apostrophe of Balaam addressed to the Kenite (Num. 24 : 21), 'Strong is thy habitation, and thou settest thy nest in the crag' (בַּסֶּלַע קִנֶּךָ); and again in the tender words addressed in the Song (2 : 14) to the beloved one, 'O my dove, in the clefts of the crag (בְּחַגְוֵי הַסֶּלַע), in the hidden recess of the step-rock (בְּסֵתֶר הַמַּדְרֵגָה[1]), show me thy countenance, let me hear thy voice.' Reference to the habits of the eagle is only to be expected, and allusion is actually made in Job 39 : 28, 'On a cliff doth she dwell (סֶלַע יִשְׁכֹּן) and lodge, on a peak of a cliff (עַל־שֶׁן־סֶלַע) and a stronghold;' and similar mention is made of the haunts of the

---
[1] On the precise meaning of this term, see what is stated at page 71 ff.

mountain-goat (Job 39:1), 'Knowest thou the time when the wild goats of the cliff (יַעֲלֵי־סָלַע) bring forth?' Significantly also Amos (6:12) sets forth the madness of sinful Israel in fancying that they could possibly pervert righteousness: 'Can horses run upon a cliff (הַיְרֻצוּן בַּסֶּלַע סוּסִים), or can any one plough the sea with oxen?'[1]

Even men might often prudently betake themselves, for safety and defence, to cliffs which are not merely lofty but most difficult of access; spots like these are naturally formed for fortresses. Allusion to the safety of such sites is made in the description given by Isaiah (33:16) of the righteous man, upright and incorruptible, '*He* shall dwell on high; his high place of security shall be the munitions of crags' (מְצָדוֹת סְלָעִים). Highly instructive in this connection is the exhortation addressed to Moab in Jer. 48:28, 'O ye that dwell in Moab, leave the city and dwell in the cliff (בַּסֶּלַע), and be like a dove that maketh her nest on the further side of the mouth of the pit.' Samson betook himself (Jud. 15:8, 11) for safety from the Philistines to a cleft of the crag of Etam (סְעִיף סֶלַע עֵיטָם); and afterwards (Jud. 20:45, 47), the remnant of the Benjaminites similarly fled to the 'crag of Rimmon' (סֶלַע הָרִמּוֹן), a rocky eminence which may still be identified.

Further monumental and historical evidence corroborating the essential meaning of the word is presented in *Sela*,[2] the name of the famous capital of Edom, since called (with like signification) *Petra*, a city of precipitous cliffs. Very instructive also is the description, in 1 Sam. 14:4, of the two opposing crags at the pass near the scene of the exploit by Jonathan and his armour-bearer.[3] A precipitous cliff, moreover, is precisely the kind of rock to afford a cool and refreshing shade in a 'weary land' (Is. 32:2); while its summit forms only too convenient a point from which an enemy might be cast down to instant destruction; see 2 Chron. 25:12; Ps. 141:6; Jer. 51:25.

It is worthy of notice that when water was miraculously provided

---

[1] Here we follow the amended reading בְּבָקָר יָם, now generally accepted instead of the objectionable בַּבְּקָרִים (a plural collective) in the Massoretic text.

[2] In 2 Kings 14:7, and Jer. 49:16, the name is given as הַסֶּלַע, but in the poetic style of Isaiah 26:1 and of Obadiah 3, simply סֶלַע, (without the article). It is doubtful whether the reference in Jud. 1:36 and Is. 42:11 is to this city.

[3] See page 116 for an examination of this passage.

NOUNS SIGNIFYING A ROCK.

for the Israelites in the wilderness at Rephidim, as recorded in Exodus, the term employed (17 : 6) to designate the object smitten is צוּר; and the same word is preserved in the later allusions to this event in Is. 48 : 21, 'Water from a hard rock (צוּר) he caused to flow down for them,' in Ps. 105 : 41, 'He opened a hard rock (צוּר), and water flowed abundantly,' and also in 114 : 8. On the other hand, in the account given in Num. (ch. 20) of the later miracle of a similar kind at Kadesh, the word used throughout is סֶלַע (see verses 8, 10, 11); which reappears in the later reference made to this event by Nehemiah (9 : 15) and his fellows in the covenant, 'Water out of a crag (מִסֶּלַע) didst thou bring forth to them.' And again, in Ps. 78 : 15, 16 (cf. also ver. 20), where reference is made to both occurrences, the two distinctive names are carefully preserved; 'He clave hard rocks (צֻרִים) in the wilderness...and brought descending streams out of a cliff' (מִסֶּלַע).[1]

While the distinction between these two terms is thus far firmly maintained in Scripture, attention must now be called to the only passage in which an interchange appears. In Judges 6 : 20, we read that the angel of Jehovah commanded Gideon to lay upon 'yonder crag'[2] (הַסֶּלַע הַלָּז) the flesh and the unleavened cakes which he had prepared; while, in the verse immediately following, we read that the flesh and the cakes were consumed by a fire which issued from 'the rock' (הַצּוּר). It seems most probable that at least one portion of the stony eminence presented an abrupt face, and thus might appropriately be designated a סֶלַע, while another aspect of the same object would equally warrant the application of the term צוּר.

It is now possible to distinguish between the different ideas before the mind of the distressed Psalmist when uttering (Ps. 31 : 3, 4) his request to Jehovah, 'Be thou to me a fortress-rock (צוּר־מָעוֹז)...For thou art my high rock and my mountain-stronghold' (סַלְעִי וּמְצוּדָתִי),

---

[1] An analogous distinction is strictly maintained by the Evangelists in their accounts of the two different occasions on which Jesus miraculously fed the multitudes. The 'baskets' in which the fragments were gathered, after the wants of the five thousand were satisfied, are throughout termed κόφινοι (see Matt. 14 : 20; Mark 6 : 43; Luke 9 : 17; John 6 : 13); whereas those which were employed after the feeding of the four thousand, are, with similar persistency, called σπυρίδες by the two narrators who record this event (Matt. 15 : 37; Mark 8 : 8). Jesus further preserves the distinction when afterwards referring to both events together (Matt. 16 : 9, 10; Mark 8 : 19, 20).

[2] The common rendering, 'this rock,' is obviously inexact.

Like distinction is to be observed in Isaiah's prediction (2 : 21) of the flight of guilty and conscience-smitten idolaters from God's revelation of wrath, 'to go into the holes of the rocks (נִקְרוֹת הַצֻּרִים) and into the clefts of the crags' (סְעִפֵי הַסְּלָעִים); and similarly again in Ps. 71 : 3, 'Be thou to me a rock-dwelling (צוּר מָעוֹן) for constant resort; thou hast given commandment to save me, for thou art my high rock and my stronghold' (סַלְעִי וּמְצוּדָתִי).

d. Though mostly found in its proper and original meaning of a 'tooth,' (as Ex. 21 : 24, 27 ; Lev. 24 : 20 ; Deut. 19 : 21, etc.), שֵׁן, by an obvious metaphor, has come to signify a rocky peak,[1] rising from what already forms a crag. We meet with it in the account of Jonathan's bold and successful exploit in attacking the Philistine station near Michmash, attended solely by his armour-bearer. 'Between the passes which Jonathan sought to cross unto the garrison of the Philistines, [there is] the point of a crag (שֵׁן הַסֶּלַע) on one side, and the point of a crag on the other side. The one peak (הַשֵּׁן הָאֶחָד) [is] a column (מָצוּק) on the north, opposite to Michmash, while the other [is] on the south, opposite Gibeah,' 1 Sam. 14 : 4. The term is fitly introduced once more in Job 39 : 28, in a description of the eagle's haunt; 'On a crag (סֶלַע) doth he dwell and lodge, on a peak of a crag (עַל־שֶׁן־סֶלַע) and a rock-fortress' (מְצוּדָה).

---

[1] Cf. the analogous application of 'dent,' in French, to denote certain Alpine peaks ('Dent Blanche,' 'Dent du Midi').

17. Nouns signifying a Rod, Stick, or Staff.

a. מַקֵּל,   *b.* מִשְׁעֶנֶת,   *c.* מַטֶּה,[1]   *d.* שֵׁבֶט.[1]

a. The noun מַקֵּל (plur. מַקְלוֹת) is evidently applied merely to (1) a *common stick* or rod, of raw or unseasoned wood, fairly straight and smooth, freshly formed from a branch or the stem of a tree, and only slightly dressed in order to adapt it for the special purpose it is meant to serve. Further, (2) it is essentially light, and thus easily handled, (3) not very long, though probably beyond the stature of a man, and (4) only meant for temporary use,[2] hence at once discarded as a thing of little value when the need for it is past. Such a plain and homely stick was commonly prepared for use during a journey by a traveller, as a support when he felt weak and weary, but it would be laid aside as useless after his destination had been reached.

The earliest occurrence of this term is in the history of Jacob, where we read (Gen. 30 : 37-41) that, to increase the number of his flocks as speedily as possible, he placed before the cattle, in their water-troughs, rods (מַקְלוֹת) that he had prepared and partly peeled. Later, this patriarch, returning from his long sojourn with Laban, and recounting the enriching mercies of the Lord, displayed since his departure from his father's house, gratefully acknowledges, ' With my stick (בְּמַקְלִי) I crossed this Jordan, and now I have become two companies ' (Gen. 32 : 10). And one of the directions given to the Israelites regarding the first celebration of the Passover, in Egypt, on the eve of their departure, runs as follows, ' Thus shall ye eat it, —[with] your loins girded, your sandals on your feet, and your stick

---

[1] In the following discussion, as will be seen, we merely touch incidentally on the application of מַטֶּה and שֵׁבֶט to signify a ' tribe ' of Israel.

[2] Contrast, in this respect, the other terms to be considered afterwards.

(מַקֶּלְכֶם) in your hand' (Ex. 12 : 11). This term is likewise used to designate the rough and homely stick[1] (מַקֵּל, 1 Sam. 17 : 40) which David carried when advancing to attack Goliath. Deeming himself insulted by the mean appearance of the Hebrew champion, bearing still meaner weapons, scornfully the giant asks, 'Am I a dog, that thou comest unto me with common sticks' (בְּמַקְלוֹת)? It was with such a temporary travelling-stick (מַקֵּל) that the perverse Balaam smote[2] his ass (Num. 22 : 27). When again we read in an early prophecy of Jeremiah (1 : 11) that the seer beheld in vision an almond-stick (מַקֵּל שָׁקֵד), we are certainly to understand that its wood must have been viewed as still fresh[3] and 'green'; and when, once more, we find the Lord complaining of his people, through the prophet Hosea (4 : 12), that in their apostasy they do not enquire of him but ask at their stock (עֵץ), while their stick (מַקֵּל) declares to them, it is easy to perceive the value at which their oracles are appraised. All that we have now observed enables us to read aright the prophecy in Zechariah 11 : 3-14, where, though foolish and negligent shepherds figure largely, the mention of the two staves, called Beauty and Binders, should not allow us to assume that these are shepherds' staves; as מַקֵּל is the term employed in both cases (see verses 7, 10, 14), we must conclude that rods of unseasoned wood, roughly and hastily prepared from trees growing at hand, are all that may be understood as meant.

b. That מִשְׁעֶנֶת signifies a *staff*, properly so called, constantly employed[4] as a means of support, especially for the aged and infirm, but even for younger persons who are weak, might at once be inferred from a consideration of its root and its cognate derivatives.[5]

---

[1] The 'stick' which David carried in the combat with the giant would not appear to mean his shepherd-staff, for which, as we shall see, the proper term is שֵׁבֶט; this he would surely leave at home.

[2] This is the only instance in which we read of the מַקֵּל as used in smiting; but the prophet had no other weapon. As will be shown, a שֵׁבֶט was the common instrument for chastisement.

[3] Contrast the application of מַטֶּה (to be afterwards explained) to designate Aaron's rod that miraculously budded (Numbers, chap. 17).

[4] In this respect especially, מִשְׁעֶנֶת differs from the temporary מַקֵּל.

[5] The Niphal נִשְׁעַן is constantly used in the sense of leaning for support, as in 2 Sam. 1 : 6; 2 Kings 5 : 18; Isa. 10 : 20; 2 Chron. 13 : 18, etc. The kindred

NOUNS SIGNIFYING A ROD OR STAFF.

We must further conclude that the מִשְׁעֶנֶת, of necessity, is not slim and frail, but sufficiently strong to sustain considerable weight. A careful survey of the passages in which the term occurs will make this plain.

In the law of Moses (Ex. 21 : 18, 19) it was enacted that when a man was injured by his neighbour in a fight, and had to keep his bed, if he rose again and walked abroad upon his staff (מִשְׁעַנְתּוֹ), then he that smote him should be quit,—only, he had to pay for the loss of the other's time, and cause him to be completely healed. And a beautiful prophecy in Zech. 8 : 4 declared, 'Old men and old women shall yet sit in the streets of Jerusalem, each with his staff (מִשְׁעַנְתּוֹ) in his hand, for very age.' The messenger whom Sennacherib sent to Jerusalem, warning Hezekiah to submit, insultingly asked, 'On whom dost thou trust that thou hast rebelled against me ? Now, behold, thou trustest upon the staff of this bruised reed (עַל־מִשְׁעֶנֶת הַקָּנֶה הָרָצוּץ הַזֶּה),—upon Egypt,—on which, if a man lean, it will go into his hand and pierce it' (2 Kings 18 : 21, Isa. 36 : 6) ; the irony involved in speaking of a 'reed-staff,'—broken, too—is masterly. Ezekiel (29 : 6, 7), uttering his prophecy against Egypt, employs like language, 'All the inhabitants of Egypt shall know that I am Jehovah, because they have been a staff of reed (מִשְׁעֶנֶת קָנֶה) to the house of Israel. When they take hold of thee with the hand, thou breakest and dost rend all their hand (פַּף[1]) ; and when they lean on thee, thou dost break, and causest all their loins to quake.'[2]

Attention must likewise be called to the staff (מִשְׁעֶנֶת) usually, it would appear, carried by Elisha, who, however, on one special occasion (2 Kings 4 : 29, 31), sent it by the hands of Gehazi in the hope that it might avail to revivify the son of the pious and hospitable Shunammite woman. This allusion to the prophet's wont in carrying a staff may safely warrant the conclusion that this man of God was not exceptionally vigorous.

---

nouns מִשְׁעָן (2 Sam. 22 : 19 ; Ps. 18 : 19, etc.), and מַשְׁעֵנָה (Isa. 3 : 1) bear the more general sense of a *direct and immediate support*, prop or stay. (Compare the use of מַטֶּה in Psalm 105 : 16 ; Ezek. 4 : 16 ; 5 : 16 ; 14 : 13, and Lev. 26 : 26, as afterwards explained).

[1] This reading seems preferable (cf. Is. 36 : 6, cited above) to the Massoretic כָּתֵף ('shoulder,' which would surely be less likely to suffer than the hand).

[2] With recent critics, we take וְהִכְמַעְדְתָּ to be the true reading (cf. Ps. 69 : 24) instead of the Massoretic וְהַעֲמַדְתָּ, which does not suit the context.

c. The noun מַטֶּה may best, perhaps, be rendered *rod*, especially a rod indicative of office or authority. But, though an emblem of superiority, it does not symbolise supreme authority,[1] but merely middle rank. Some points may first be noted, chiefly regarding its material and form.

(1) The derivation of the term (from נָטָה 'to extend'), leads us to regard the מַטֶּה as a straight rod of considerable length, beyond the average height of men; we must not think of it as short or insignificant. (2) It was made of dried or seasoned wood (thus differing from מַקֵּל), prepared with care, and—though we find no actual proof of this—probably even carved or ornamented. (3) Hence, the מַטֶּה was not made for merely temporary ends, like a מַקֵּל, but was designed for constant and important use. (4) Though long and somewhat slender, it at least was moderately strong; the term, indeed, sometimes appears associated with another which expressly emphasises this idea (thus, מַטֵּה עֹז), though the combination may point, figuratively, to strong rule, rather than the material strength of the rod itself. Such a rod, habitually borne by one whose dignity and authority it symbolised, could not conveniently be heavy; nor was strength essential.[2] Hence, we do not find it mentioned, like מִשְׁעֶנֶת, as used by the aged or infirm for a support. Neither is it, though an emblem of superior position and authority, ordinarily used in chastisement.[1] In other words, the מַטֶּה was a token of administrative rather than executive authority.

Perhaps it is primarily as a silent symbol of considerable dignity or social rank that מַטֶּה must be regarded. Like the gold-headed cane with us in bygone days, which marked its bearer as belonging to the better class, it was a token—quietly significant—that he who carried it was a superior,—one of good position in the social scale. More commonly, however, like a verger's rod, it symbolised authority, administrative power. The power might not be painfully obtruded on the persons under him, but it was manifestly present,—visible, if not in active exercise. The ruler's rod might sometimes touch the shoulders of the subject ones, but this was mainly meant as a reminder of their lot and as a stimulus to strenuous toil,—not

---

[1] Contrast what is afterwards explained regarding שֵׁבֶט.

[2] Contrast what has been said regarding מִשְׁעֶנֶת, and also what will afterwards be shown regarding שֵׁבֶט.

so much as a castigation, which the מַטֶּה, from its peculiar character, was but ill fitted to inflict.

It is significant that Judah (Gen. 38 : 18, 25), as a man of rank, wore a signet-ring (חֹתֶמֶת), suspended by the usual cord (פָּתִיל); he also bore a rod (מַטֶּה),—all emblems of superiority or social eminence, the last not being least. Such a rod[1] surely could not have been of common make; a rod intended, by its mere appearance, quietly to indicate superiority in him who bears it, must itself look anything but mean. Let us observe, besides, that Judah gave away this rod of dignity, as something certainly not indispensable; he had no real need of it as a support (cf. מִשְׁעֶנֶת), though it was useful and becoming, as a mark of rank.

But far more noteworthy, in many ways, was Moses' rod (מַטֶּה). Its earliest mention, in the account of the theophany at Horeb (Ex. 4 : 2, 4), leads us at once, apart from other facts, to think of him who carried it as not a common shepherd—for the מַטֶּה does not mean a shepherd's staff—but as (naturally) holding a position of superiority in Jethro's house. When he is bidden go to Pharaoh, he is told to take with him that very rod (4 : 17). An emblem of authority it still remains, though in another sphere; but this authority becomes, perhaps, more clearly intermediary. Moses himself is honoured— very highly honoured—only, his position is still that of a subordinate,[2] for he is under God as the Supreme, and thus the rod is called 'the rod of God' (מַטֵּה הָאֱלֹהִים, Exod. 4 : 20; 17 : 9). This designation really gives a key to Moses' life and work. To Pharaoh, he appears clothed with authority, but it is divine authority; words are given him to speak to Pharaoh, so that he becomes Jehovah's prophet,[3] as when he declares, 'The Lord God of the Hebrews hath sent me unto thee' (Exod. 7 : 16). Moses, moreover, carries in his hand his 'rod of God,' that Pharaoh may not merely hear but also see.

To Israel also, Moses ever is the visible superior. He speaks and acts with all authority, yet this authority is evidently not inherent, but derived. The great lawgiver is but God's servant, at the most;

---

[1] The common rendering ('staff') is apt to convey a wrong impression.

[2] Consider the contrast drawn in the Epistle to the Hebrews (3 : 5, 6), 'Moses certainly was faithful in all his [i. e. God's] house, as a servant......but Christ as a son, over his house.'

[3] The Hebrew prophet was essentially God's spokesman or mouth-piece.

and here, once more, 'the rod of God' told its own tale to Israel, visibly declaring the divine authority of Moses. To a nation of grown children, living by sense of sight rather than by the eye of faith, this 'rod of God' by means of which so many miracles were wrought (Ex. 8 : 1, 12, 13 ; 9 : 23 ; 10 : 13 ; 14 : 16, etc.) was evidently meant to guide the people's thoughts beyond itself and him who bore it, to the real Leader, with supreme command,—the heavenly King.[1]

We further read of Aaron's rod (מַטֶּה), and here, once more, the circumstances are significant. Jehovah said to Moses, ' See, I have made thee a god to Pharaoh, while Aaron thy brother shall be thy prophet. *Thou* shalt speak all that I have commanded thee, but Aaron thy brother shall speak unto Pharaoh' (Exod. 7 : 1, 2). For the time being, Moses is thus to bear the highest honour, while his brother is to be his intermediary. Accordingly, while Moses stands in Pharaoh's presence, clothed with the highest dignity, Aaron, as his subordinate, now bears a rod (מַטֶּה) to indicate that he, too, has authority, though not the highest. Pharaoh obviously understands all this, and the details of the succeeding history confirm this view. For now, it is not Moses who works miracles, but Aaron (Exod. 7 : 17, 19 ; 8 : 1, 12, 13), using his rod, the fitting emblem of authority and power. In this case likewise, we may safely take for granted that the mere appearance of the rod was calculated to command respect.

A later incident throws still more light upon this subject. After Korah, Dathan and Abiram were destroyed, and their rebellion was put down, Moses received command (Num. 17 : 16 ff.) that all the leaders of the tribes should take a rod (מַטֶּה), and that each prince should write his name upon his own, Aaron's name, however, being inscribed upon the rod which represented his own tribe. Of these twelve rods, laid up before Jehovah in the tabernacle overnight, Aaron's was found next day in blossom, and with almonds which it had produced.

Certain points claim our attention here. First, the production of the blossoms and the fruit was wonderful,—a miracle, because the process was so rapid ; still more wonderful was it that these should

---

[1] We shall see hereafter that the שֵׁבֶט (sceptre) was the rod of royal rule.

NOUNS SIGNIFYING A ROD OR STAFF. 123

grow from seasoned wood,—a stem or branch that had been peeled and dried, as was the case with the מַטֶּה. Next, the מַטֶּה anew presents us with the notion of authority and rule—direction or administration carried on by leaders—though of intermediate character. But further, we now clearly see, in this important incident, *organization*, orderly arrangement of the individuals and families which formed the tribes.[1]

Even on the battle-field, Jonathan carried a rod (מַטֶּה, 1 Sam. 14 : 27, 43). On first thought, this might seem quite out of place—a dangerous encumbrance, to be quickly cast aside in favour of a spear. But when we think of Jonathan's position as the son of Saul, clothed with authority, and yet under authority—commanding others under him, yet under a superior himself—we see the fitness of the מַטֶּה as a token, readily perceptible, of his position in relation to his father as the king, and to the people whom he led.

The conceptions we have now been led to form regarding מַטֶּה will enable us to read some other passages, not in themselves quite clear, with the persuasion that we know what must be meant. Mic. 6 : 9 at best is difficult to understand in its entirety, but we may at least be confident that the words מַטֶּה שִׁמְעוּ 'hear ye [the] rod,' counsel submission to constituted authority. Again, when Isaiah (9 : 3), addressing the Lord in gladness of heart, exclaims, 'The rod [2] of his back ([3] שִׁכְמוֹ מַטֶּה) hast thou broken,' we are to understand by this the symbol of superiority in the hands of an overseer or taskmaster who used it, not so much for a slight castigation, as rather to rouse the enslaved toilers to renewed energy, when they seemed to slacken their exhausting efforts. A similar reference to organized rule presents itself in Is. 14 : 5, where the prophet records the Lord's de-

---

[1] Waiving fuller consideration of מַטֶּה and שֵׁבֶט as applied to a 'tribe' of Israel, we may merely allude to the acute observation of S. D. Luzzatto (see his בית האוצר, Przemysl, 1888, page 146), that the twelve sons of Jacob, the heads or progenitors, are called שְׁבָטִים, not מַטּוֹת, but the entire *descendants* of each שֵׁבֶט together form a מַטֶּה. This distinction, as we shall see presently, accords with that which obtains between these same terms when used to signify a 'rod.'

[2] It will be observed that this prophet naturally has frequent occasion to employ the term in speaking of the organized tyranny rampant in his days.

[3] שְׁכֶם denotes the upper portion of the back, below the neck and between the shoulder-blades; whereas כָּתֵף (*du.* כְּתֵפַיִם) is applied to the top of the arm, outward from the ear.

liverance of his oppressed people, 'Jehovah hath broken the rod of unrighteous men' (שָׁבַר מַטֵּה רְשָׁעִים). Particularly instructive are the words of Ezekiel (7 : 11), 'Wrong-doing hath risen up into a rod of unrighteousness'[1] (קָם לְמַטֵּה רֶשַׁע); the prophet thereby obviously meant that robbery combined with violence had become established in the form of a constant tyranny over the oppressed. See also Isa. 10 : 5, 15, 24, 26.

This is likewise the stage at which we may perhaps most fully appreciate the exact force of the figurative language employed in Ps. 105 : 16, where reference is made to the famine in the time of Joseph as a visitation from the Lord; 'the whole rod of bread he brake' (כָּל־מַטֵּה־לֶחֶם שָׁבָר). Read in the light we have now obtained, this remarkable language must plainly be held to signify the utter disorganization and final collapse of all the ordinary arrangements for the supply and distribution of food in a community.[2] The same figure is introduced in Ezek. 4 : 16, where the prophet, speaking in the name of Jehovah, thus declares, 'Behold, I will break the rod of bread (הִנְנִי שֹׁבֵר מַטֵּה־לֶחֶם) in Jerusalem, and they shall eat bread by weight;' and again in 5 : 16, 'Famine will I increase upon you, and I will break for you the rod of bread' (מַטֵּה־לֶחֶם); and once more in 14 : 13, 'I will break the rod of bread;' see also Lev. 26 : 26. The ordinary English renderings, however, must not be allowed to prevent us from observing that the metaphor and the associated idea presented in these passages are different from what we find in Isa. 3 : 1, where the prophet proclaims the advent of famine and distress; 'Behold, the Lord, Jehovah of hosts, doth remove staff and stay (מַשְׁעֵן וּמַשְׁעֵנָה) from Jerusalem and from Judah, the whole staff of bread (מִשְׁעַן־לֶחֶם) and the whole staff of water' (מִשְׁעַן־מָיִם). Obviously, bread and water are here figuratively set forth as the direct *supports* of life.

Other passages in which מַטֶּה occurs will be conveniently considered afterwards.

---

[1] Such utterances present excellent illustrations of the essentially concrete form in which the ancient Hebrews gave expression to their thoughts; abstract or general terms are comparatively rare.

[2] In modern warfare, the importance of an efficient commissariat is distinctly recognised; defect in this department may, in presence of the enemy, be fraught with danger and even ensure defeat.

NOUNS SIGNIFYING A ROD OR STAFF.

d. The term שֵׁבֶט,—perhaps best rendered as a 'stout [strong] rod,' or sometimes 'sceptre,'—can be most advantageously regarded in its relation to מַטֶּה, from which it differs in several important particulars.

1. The שֵׁבֶט was comparatively short, while the מַטֶּה, as we have shown, was of considerable length. Hence, we do not find a שֵׁבֶט used, even exceptionally, as a support; it was not long enough to reach from the middle of the human body to the ground. It did not support the hand; the hand supported it.

2. Of the two, a שֵׁבֶט was the thicker and especially the stronger, yet it was not heavy, so as to be burdensome.

3. The שֵׁבֶט, being stronger as well shorter, was more fitted than the מַטֶּה for some serviceable ends; the latter was more fit for show than use. Hence, as has been already remarked, a שֵׁבֶט or short and stout rod is, naturally, most frequently employed as an instrument for chastisement; for, whereas the מַטֶּה served mainly as a visible emblem of superior authority or of administrative power, the שֵׁבֶט was especially both a token of executive power and a means of making this power felt by others. It was thus eminently an executive instrument.

4. Accordingly, שֵׁבֶט becomes the proper term for a 'sceptre,'[1] as the emblem of supreme or regal power, executive as well as judicial. It is thus likewise the fit and proper designation for the staff of a shepherd, who obviously exercises supreme control over his flock.

The force of these remarks will be more distinctly felt on observing the actual usage of the term in some passages; let us first note cases in which שֵׁבֶט comes before us as a means of inflicting bodily pain or chastisement.

In Ex. 21 : 20, we read the simple enactment, 'Whenever a man smites his manservant or his maidservant with the rod (בַּשֵּׁבֶט), and he dies under his hand, he shall certainly be avenged.' In the gracious message from the Lord, sent through Nathan the prophet to David regarding his son, we find these words (2 Sam. 7 : 14), 'Whenever he acts perversely, then will I correct him with the rod of men' (בְּשֵׁבֶט אֲנָשִׁים); while the same idea is presented in the more fully expanded terms of the new covenant as found in Ps. 89 : 32, 'If they profane my statutes and keep not my commandments, then will I

---

[1] The later form שַׁרְבִיט occurs in Esther 4 : 11; 5 : 2; 8 : 4.

visit their transgression with a rod' (בְּשֵׁבֶט). More plain and pointed reference to corporal correction meets us in the pithy proverb, 'In the lips of a discerning man, wisdom is found, but a rod (שֵׁבֶט) is for the back of one that lacketh understanding' (Prov. 10 : 13); 'He that spareth his rod (שִׁבְטוֹ) hateth his son' (13 : 24); '[Though] stubborn folly (אִוֶּלֶת [1]) is bound up in the heart of a youth, [yet] the rod of correction (שֵׁבֶט מוּסָר) will drive it far from him' (22 : 15); 'Do not withhold correction from a youth; when thou smitest him with the rod (כִּי תַכֶּנּוּ בַשֵּׁבֶט), he shall not die. Thou thyself shalt smite him with the rod (אַתָּה בַּשֵּׁבֶט תַּכֶּנּוּ), and shalt deliver his soul from Sheol' (23 : 13, 14); 'A whip for the horse, a bridle for the ass, and a rod for the back of [talkative] fools' (שֵׁבֶט לְגֵו כְּסִילִים [1], 26 : 3); 'A rod and reproof (שֵׁבֶט וְתוֹכַחַת) give wisdom' (29 : 15). See also Isa. 9 : 3; 14 : 29; Mic. 4 : 14.

We are now able to realise the risk and to appreciate the bravery of Benaiah, in attacking an Egyptian armed with a spear (2 Sam. 23 : 21; 1 Chr. 11 : 23), 'He went down to him with a rod (בַּשֵּׁבֶט) and tore the spear out of the hand of the Egyptian, and slew him with his own spear.' A short (though stout) rod like the שֵׁבֶט was indeed but a sorry means of attack and defence against a spear-armed foe.

Sufficiently plain, though less explicit, are some other passages in which שֵׁבֶט is used metaphorically, as Job 9 : 34, where the sufferer, speaking of the Lord's dealings, entreats, 'Let him remove his rod (שִׁבְטוֹ) from upon me,' and 21 : 9, where, describing the wicked in their prosperity, he says, 'Their houses are safe from fear (מִפַּחַד) neither is the rod of God (שֵׁבֶט אֱלוֹהַּ) upon them;' also Lam. 3 : 1, 'I am the strong man [that] hath seen affliction by the rod of his wrath' (בְּשֵׁבֶט עֶבְרָתוֹ). Reference to iniquitous use of the castigating rod is made in the psalmist's confident and hopeful words (Ps. 125 : 3), 'The rod of unrighteousness (שֵׁבֶט הָרֶשַׁע) shall not rest upon the lot of the righteous ones, lest the righteous put forth their hands unto iniquity.'

But further, the application of the term שֵׁבֶט to a shepherd's rod brings out distinctly the idea of supreme or absolute authority and power. The shepherd exercises undisputed sway over his flock, and holds them in complete control. Within his own domain, he is an

---

[1] See the remarks already made at pages 29 and 31.

NOUNS SIGNIFYING A ROD OR STAFF.

'uncrowned king,' whose sceptre is his rod.[1] To 'pass under the rod,' even when the immediate object was to count the sheep (as in Lev. 27 : 32), always implied subjection to the shepherd's sway, and in this light we must read the figurative language of Ezekiel (20 : 37) declaring God's designs for good in Israel, when he subdues them to himself; 'I will plead with you, and I will make you to pass under the rod (וְהַעֲבַרְתִּי אֶתְכֶם תַּחַת הַשָּׁבֶט), and will bring you into the bond of the covenant.' The same figure of sovereign but salutary sway exercised by a shepherd forms the basis of Micah's entreaty to the Lord for scattered Israel (7 : 14), 'Tend thy people with thy rod (בְּשִׁבְטֶךָ), the flock of thine inheritance, that dwelleth alone.' And again, the familiar words of the shepherd-psalm (23 : 4) should now convey more definite ideas of their sense, 'Thy shepherd-rod and thy supporting staff (שִׁבְטְךָ וּמִשְׁעַנְתֶּךָ)—*they* comfort me;' because the Lord is at once the sovereign ruler, corrector, and protector, as well as the guide of his peculiar people.

Such passages, illustrating the use of שֵׁבֶט as the rod of superior judicial authority and punitive power, amply prepare us for finally regarding the highest application of the term to designate a regal rod,—the sceptre of a king. A few passages may be cited.

The words of Psalm 45 : 7 are unmistakable, 'The sceptre of thy kingdom (שֵׁבֶט מַלְכוּתֶךָ) is a sceptre of rectitude;' while supreme and irresistible power over earthly kings is clearly affirmed in the words of Psalm 2 : 9, addressed to the Messianic King, 'Thou shalt break them with an iron sceptre (תְּרֹעֵם בְּשֵׁבֶט בַּרְזֶל); like a potter's vessel shalt thou dash them in pieces.' It is also obvious that, in Gen. 49 : 10, the departure of 'the sceptre from Judah' signifies the loss of royalty or sovereignty; and similarly, when it is declared in Zech. 10 : 11 that 'the sceptre of Egypt shall depart' (שֵׁבֶט מִצְרַיִם יָסוּר), we must thereby understand the conquest of the land, and hence the loss of national independence.

---

[1] In the East, a shepherd carries *two* sticks. The first is a short, straight, and strong oaken club (the שֵׁבֶט), used for offensive and defensive purposes, having a knob at the outer end, while a string is passed through the handle-end, that the instrument may thereby be hung at the side when not in use. The second stick, which is thinner, and curved at the upper end, is about the height of the shepherd himself, who uses it as a staff (a מִשְׁעֶנֶת), for support in walking, or in clambering among rocks.

We are now able to read, with some degree of confidence that we understand their meaning, certain other passages in which two of the synonymous terms now discussed are combined.

In Isa. 28:27, whatever obscurity may attach to one's ideas concerning the different kinds of seed mentioned, there should be somewhat definite conceptions regarding the threshing instruments employed, when we read that 'with a [long and light] rod (בְּמַטֶּה) must vetches be beaten out, but cummin with a [short and stout] stick' (בַּשֵּׁבֶט). The 'vetches' are thus more easily threshed than cummin, which has harder husks.

In Isa. 10:24, 25, words of comfort are addressed to Israel: 'O my people that dwellest in Zion, be not afraid of Assyria that shall smite thee with the [castigating] rod (בַּשֵּׁבֶט) and shall lift up his rod [of settled authority] over thee (יִשָּׂא עָלֶיךָ מַטֵּהוּ), in the manner of Egypt. For yet a very little while, and indignation shall cease.' These words point, not to mere castigation, but this combined with organized dominion over a subjugated Israel, such as their fathers had experienced in Egypt. And similarly we must understand a more obscure expression in a previous verse (5), 'Woe to the Assyrian, the [chastising] rod of mine anger (שֵׁבֶט אַפִּי), while the rod [of settled government] which[1] is in their hand (מַטֶּה־הוּא בְיָדָם) is mine indignation!'

The conclusions drawn from passages already considered are further confirmed by the language employed in other instances. Isa. 14:5 forms a portion of the divine sentence pronounced against Babylon, 'Jehovah hath broken the [directing] rod of the unrighteous ones (מַטֵּה רְשָׁעִים), and the sceptre of those holding supreme sway' (שֵׁבֶט מֹשְׁלִים); here it is of importance to mark that the verb מָשַׁל, denoting rule in its highest form, is properly associated with its symbol שֵׁבֶט. Still stronger confirmation is afforded by Ezekiel 19:10-14, though the passage as a whole continues to present difficulties, 'Thy mother [is] like a vine...and she had [straight] strong rods (מַטּוֹת עֹז) [which became] sceptres of those who bear supreme sway (שִׁבְטֵי מֹשְׁלִים)...But she was plucked up in fury...and each of her strong [thin] rods (מַטֵּה עֻזָּהּ[2] יָבֵשׁוּ) withered; fire devoured it.

---

[1] On the peculiar construction of the relative here, see the author's Introduction to Biblical Hebrew, page 223.

[2] This individualising construction (a plural predicate with a subject in the

And now she is planted in the wilderness...and there is not in her a strong [light] rod (מַטֵּה עֹז), a sceptre for supreme rule' (שֵׁבֶט לִמְשׁוֹל). Specially significant and instructive for us is the relation, evident in these verses, subsisting between the מַטֶּה and the שֵׁבֶט, and the conjunction of the latter with מָשַׁל.

The foregoing results seem to warrant an emendation in the Massoretic text of Jud. 5 : 14 b, where we should probably read, 'Out of Machir came down lawgivers (מְחֹקְקִים), and out of Zebulon those who rule supreme with the sceptre' (מֹשְׁלִים [1] בַּשֵּׁבֶט).

We are further enabled to read with increased precision of perception a passage in a long prophecy of Jeremiah (48 : 17) abounding in obscure allusions.[2] The fall of Moab is the theme throughout. In prophetic vision the cry is raised, 'How is the strong rod [of settled but subordinate authority] broken, the [rough] stick [of] boasting!' (נִשְׁבַּר מַטֵּה־עֹז מַקֵּל תִּפְאָרָה). It is remarkable that מַטֶּה (not שֵׁבֶט) is the term selected here to mark apparently the highest form of rule in Moab. Must we thence infer that Moab was at this time but a vassal-state, deprived of its own king? Historical research may yet throw light upon this point in Moab's past. We know, however, that the whole of Syria was then the battle-ground on which the hosts of Egypt on the one hand, and the armies of Chaldea on the other, met in the struggle for supremacy. Thus Moab, like all other nations round about, fell under the dominion now of the old, now of the new great monarchy. Its independence was completely lost.

But the concluding words in ver. 17 are likewise noteworthy, 'the [roughly dressed] stick [of] boasting.' That this, and not such an expression as 'the rod of beauty,' is something like the proper rendering, becomes further evident when we read the call addressed in the very next verse to the inhabitants of various cities in the land.

---

singular) is more rare (Ezek. 48 : 19 ; Isa. 16 : 4) than the converse arrangement of a plural subject with a singular predicate (Jer. 50 : 42 ; Zech. 11 : 5 ; Psalm 66 : 3 ; 119 : 137, etc.).

[1] Not מֹשְׁכִים בְּשֵׁבֶט סֹפֵר, for which the rendering of the A. V. is 'they that handle the pen of the writer,' while our Revisers prefer to translate, 'they that handle the marshal's staff,' placing in the margin, 'they that handle the staff of the scribe.' But סֹפֵר should rather form the first word of the next verse.

[2] Jeremiah adapted and amplified prophecies which were previously uttered by Isaiah (chapters 15, 16 and 24).

'Come down from [thy] glory (רְדִי מִכָּבוֹד), O daughter that dost inhabit Dibon,' and more plainly in verse 29, 'We have heard of the haughtiness of Moab (גְאוֹן־מוֹאָב); he is very haughty (גֵּאֶה מְאֹד); his loftiness and his haughtiness and his hauteur (גַּבְהוֹ וּגְאוֹנוֹ וְגַאֲוָתוֹ), and his high-mindedness' (רָם לִבּוֹ). How expressive is the contrast in the combination here! Moab is fitly figured by a stick of green wood,—rough and raw and rudely dressed; yet this stick is the essence and embodiment [1] of pride.

Passages still awaiting elucidation are Isa. 30:31, 32, and Ezek. 21:15-18 [verses 10-12 in English]. But the Massoretic text in both cases evidently requires correction before exegesis need be attempted. We must thus wait until the labours of critics shall have secured for us at least more probable and intelligible readings than we now possess.

---

[1] The form מַקֵּל (evidently retained in the absolute state before תִּפְאָרָה, and thus in apposition) seems to present this view.

18. Nouns denoting Ashes.

a. אֵפֶר. *b.* דֶּשֶׁן.

a. The most common Hebrew term for 'ashes,' אֵפֶר, is a collective noun, signifying the finer mineral elements remaining unconsumed (or incombustible) after fire has finished its destructive and transforming work. Among the Jews, such ashes obviously would be charcoal dust (as wood was used for fuel), of grey or whitish hue; see the allusion in Psalm 147 : 16. But the character of the ashes would vary through the admixture of other similarly unconsumed remains, which might even be those of animals (Num. 19 : 9, 10, 17). As fatty and other animal substances disappeared during the process of combustion, this ash-dust is essentially fine, light, and dry. Rabbinical writers say that אֵפֶר was what had been passed through a sieve.

The simplest Scripture illustration, exhibiting the word in its primary sense, is found in the prophecy against the king of Tyre delivered by Ezekiel (28 : 18), who thus foretells the ruin of the famous merchant city, 'Because of the multitude of thine iniquities,...I will bring forth fire from the midst of thee, and it shall devour thee, and I will bring thee to ashes' (לְאֵפֶר אֱתָנְךָ). An excellent example of composite ashes is presented by those of the red heifer, which was burned in its entirety—'her skin, and her flesh, and her blood, and her dung' (Num. 19 : 5)—with some cedar-wood, and hyssop, and scarlet, all cast into the fire to be consumed together; and though the resultant ashes (אֵפֶר ver. 9, 10 [1]), which were prepared for pur-

---

[1] To these we must also add verse 17, where, instead of מֵעֲפַר—which is inappropriate, inasmuch as עָפָר (see the following group of synonyms) signifies the dust constituting the soil (viz. אֲדָמָה)—we should read מֵאֵפֶר, of which the Massoretic form is obviously a corruption. Similarly erroneous substitution by transcribers, of ע for א, is seen in 2 Samuel 18 : 3 (first part), 1 Kings 1 : 18 (second part) where עַתָּה should be אַתָּה; in 1 Sam. 1 : 10, Jerem. 6 : 10 etc., we further

poses of purification afterwards, are called those of the red heifer, as forming the most important portion of the whole, it must not be forgotten that these were really a mixture of several different elements.

In many other passages, however, אֵפֶר is introduced in a secondary or figurative sense, as a token of humiliation or self-abasement. The words used by Abraham when interceding with the Lord on behalf of Sodom and Gomorrah (Gen. 18 : 27) will readily come to mind, 'Behold now, I have taken it upon me to speak to my Lord, though I am [but] dust and ashes' (עָפָר וָאֵפֶר). We read, later, of Tamar (2 Sam. 13 : 19) showing her dire distress by putting ashes (אֵפֶר) on her head and by rending the peculiar garment which she wore as an unmarried daughter of the king. Specially noteworthy in this connection is the evident play upon words by Isaiah (see 61 : 3) when prefiguring the advent of the Messiah 'to give a garland instead of ashes' (פְּאֵר תַּחַת אֵפֶר). It is recorded (Esther 4 : 1) that Mordecai revealed his deep sense of the danger threatening the whole Jewish race through the machinations of Haman, by clothing himself in sackcloth and ashes (שַׂק וָאֵפֶר), while many others followed his example (verse 3). Daniel (9 : 3) in like manner, before pouring out his grand penitential prayer for his people, humbled himself before God with fasting and sackcloth and ashes (בְּצוֹם וְשַׂק וָאֵפֶר). Job's reverence and godly fear naturally constrained him, in the day of his calamity, to like manifestations of self-abasement; hence we read (2 : 8) that when smitten with his severe bodily suffering, he took a potsherd wherewith to scrape himself, 'sitting among the ashes' (בְּתוֹךְ־הָאֵפֶר); at a later stage (30 : 19), describing his deep humiliation, he says, 'I am become like dust and ashes' (כְּעָפָר וָאֵפֶר); while his closing words (42 : 6), expressing the deepest self-abasement and contrition before the Lord, are, 'I repent upon dust and ashes' (עַל עָפָר וָאֵפֶר). See also Jon. 3 : 6 ; Is. 58 : 5. Still greater humiliation is expressed by the Psalmist (102 : 10) when he says, 'I have eaten ashes like bread' (אֵפֶר כַּלֶּחֶם אָכָלְתִּי); while Isaiah (44 : 20) briefly but significantly describes the mental and spiritual degradation of an idolater when he says, 'he feedeth upon ashes (רֹעֶה אֵפֶר), a deceived heart hath turned him aside.'

---

find עַל instead of אֶל. On the converse substitution of א for ע, see foot-note on page 36, and the remarks regarding עָפָר, in the following group of synonyms.

NOUNS DENOTING ASHES.

Regarding Jerem. 6 : 26 ; Ezek. 27 : 30, and Mal. 4 : 3 [3 : 21 in Hebrew], see the later discussion on words signifying 'dust,' under the term עָפָר.

b. Examination of the passages in which דֶּשֶׁן occurs soon shows that the distinguishing feature of such ashes was the presence of animal fat,[1] giving a glossy, glistening look. That the main point to be considered here is the oily appearance of these 'ashes' would appear to be established by even a single passage in which a form of the cognate verb is employed, viz., the familiar words of Ps. 23 : 5, 'Thou makest my head to shine with oil' (דִּשַּׁנְתָּ בַשֶּׁמֶן רֹאשִׁי[2]); the mere anointing was obviously sufficient to produce the visible effect. Similar guidance is afforded by one of the Proverbs (15 : 30), 'The light of the eyes gladdens the heart, and a good report makes the bones shine' (תְּדַשֶּׁן־עָצֶם). The most decisive proof, however, seems to be given in Isa. 34 : 6, 7, where, in the description of judgments to fall on the inhabitants of Edom, the sword of Jehovah is depicted as 'made to shine with fat[3]' (הָדַּשְׁנָה מֵחֵלֶב), while their land was also to be soaked with blood, and 'their dust made to glisten with fat[3]' (עֲפָרָם מֵחֵלֶב יְדֻשָּׁן).

We are thus prepared for the conclusion that דֶּשֶׁן, when applied to ashes,[4] means more purely animal remains, after fire has done its work effectively; such charred remains present a shining surface, from the presence of the fat still unconsumed. Actual Scripture usage shows that דֶּשֶׁן is applied to charred remains of animals offered in sacrifice. To these remains, some fuel-ashes (אֵפֶר) could not but adhere; nevertheless this does not warrant the assertion that the דֶּשֶׁן was the ordinary altar-ashes mixed with fat dropped from sacrifices burned in the altar-fire.

The most instructive passage is Leviticus 6 : 3, 4 [verses 10, 11 in English], where directions are given regarding the removal from the altar, by the officiating priest, of the charred remains of the burnt-

---

[1] Hence the German rendering 'Fettasche,' fat ashes. Like אֵפֶר, דֶּשֶׁן is a collective noun.   [2] See the remarks already made at page 49.

[3] The common rendering, 'made fat with fatness,' is not satisfactory; it is moreover inappropriate, particularly in relation to the sword of the Lord.

[4] The term is likewise used to signify fatness as a visible indication of ease and comfort; see Jud. 9 : 9 ; Psal. 36 : 9 ; Isa. 55 : 2, etc.

offering. 'The priest shall put on his garment [of] fine white linen ......and take up the sacrificial ashes (הַדֶּשֶׁן) to which the fire shall have consumed the burnt-offering (אֲשֶׁר תֹּאכַל הָאֵשׁ אֶת־הָעֹלָה) upon the altar, and he shall put them at the side of the altar.[1] And he shall strip off his garments, and put on other garments, and shall carry out the sacrificial ashes (הַדֶּשֶׁן) to the outside of the camp, to a clean place.' Such was the regard shown to the solid remains of the sacrificial victims.

But this passage enables us to understand others in which דֶּשֶׁן is more obscurely mentioned, as 1 Kings 13 : 3, 5, where we read, first, the terms of the prophecy uttered by the prophet from Judah to the idolatrous Jeroboam, sacrificing at Bethel, 'Behold, the altar shall be rent, and the sacrificial ashes which are upon it shall be poured out' (וְנִשְׁפַּךְ הַדֶּשֶׁן אֲשֶׁר עָלָיו), and then the record of the fulfilment, 'The altar was rent, and the sacrificial ashes (הַדֶּשֶׁן) were poured out from the altar.' Again, when reference is made, in Levit. 1 : 16, to the side of the altar, eastward, as the place of the sacrificial ashes (מְקוֹם הַדֶּשֶׁן), we now know that this was the proper spot in which such remains were temporarily placed after being removed from the fire. Similarly, we may perceive the force of the allusion in Levit. 4 : 12, where directions are given regarding the disposal of the body of the bullock offered by a priest as a sin-offering for himself; this was to be carried out 'to the outside of the camp, to a clean place, to the [spot for the] outpouring of the sacrificial ashes (שֶׁפֶךְ הַדֶּשֶׁן); ...upon the [spot for the] outpouring of the sacrificial ashes it was to be burned' (עַל־שֶׁפֶךְ הַדֶּשֶׁן יִשָּׂרֵף). Finally, we may feel greater confidence in reading Jer. 31 : 39, which forms part of the prophetic description of Jerusalem as rebuilt, enlarged, and anew consecrated to the Lord : 'All the broad valley of the dead bodies and the sacrificial ashes [i. e. where these were deposited, outside the city] and all the burnings ([2] כָּל־הַשְּׂרֵפוֹת) [i. e. the place where these were performed], to the narrow torrent-valley of the Kidron,...[shall be] holy to the Lord.'

We are also able to appreciate the force of the observation that

---

[1] In Ex. 27 : 3 and Num. 4 : 13, the denominative Piël דִּשֵּׁן signifies to remove the sacrificial cinders.

[2] We take this reading rather than the erroneous Kĕthîb הַשְּׁרֵמוֹת, or the unsuitable Qĕrî הַשְּׁדֵמוֹת ('the fields').

whenever mention is made of the 'ashes' of the heifer employed in ceremonial purifications, the term employed is אֵפֶר (Num. 19 : 9, 10) —not דֶּשֶׁן, which, as we see, means animal remains reduced by fire to a 'cinder,' rather than ashes in the form of fine dust. It is evident that when only a small quantity of the ashes of the heifer were to be taken at a time, and mixed with 'running water' before this was sprinkled on the person or thing to be purified, such ashes must have been really reduced to fine dust.[1]

c. The term פִּיחַ, which has by some been supposed to indicate still another kind of 'ashes,' occurs only in Exod. 9 : 8, 9, where we read that Moses and Aaron were commanded to take from a kiln (or furnace) as much of the refuse as would fill both of their hands and throw it up into the air, that it might be scattered over all the land of Egypt; the expression employed to designate what was thus taken is פִּיחַ הַכִּבְשָׁן. But if this does mean 'the ashes of a furnace,' wherein would such ashes differ from those of an ordinary wood-fire (*i. e.* from אֵפֶר)? Difference of terms, however, surely marks some difference in things; that these Hebrew words thus rather signify 'the soot of a furnace' is more probable. This view further appears to be confirmed by the language of verse 9, where we read that this פִּיחַ was to become אָבָק (*i. e.* soft and fine powder[2]) over all the land of Egypt, producing boils and blains on man and beast. But such effects would be more naturally produced by means of soot than by wood-ash. Furnace-ash, moreover, surely is too heavy to be borne along upon the wind.

---

[1] Compare the remarks already made (pages 95, 96) on Ex. 32 : 20.
[2] See the following discussion on words signifying 'dust.'

19. Nouns denoting Dust.

a. שַׁחַק.   *b.* אָבָק.   *c.* עָפָר.

a. Beginning with one extreme, we note that of all the Hebrew words bearing this sense, שַׁחַק signifies dust in its finest, lightest, and least perceptible form. This meaning is confirmed by the common usage of the term, which nearly always indicates a light and vanishing cloud, or the sky (Deut. 33 : 26 ; Job 37 : 18, 21 ; 38 : 37, etc.) ; in one passage, however, it cannot possibly bear either sense, but must be held as signifying that exceedingly fine and light dust which is mostly imperceptible except under very favourable conditions—as when a strong ray of sunlight renders the particles visible —yet ever floating about in the atmosphere, and only settling down through the influence of moisture, or the utter absence of an exciting breeze. Such ideas evidently attach to the word as used in Is. 40 : 15, where the theme is the immensity of God in contrast with the insignificance of man. 'Behold, nations are as a drop out of a bucket, and are counted as the fine dust of a balance' (שַׁחַק מֹאזְנָיִם). Such impalpable—and even, for the most part, invisible—particles of dust on the scales make not the slightest difference in weight, so as to turn the beam ; and yet such dust is actually there.

b. Next in order comes אָבָק, which appears in only six passages ; these, however, are sufficient to illustrate the specific meaning of the term.

The greatest light is shed on this by the cognate feminine noun, even though this occurs but once—and in construction,[1] too—viz. in Cant. 3 : 6, 'Who is this, coming up out of the wilderness…perfumed with myrrh and frankincense, and with all powders of the mer-

---

[1] The absolute form, presumably, is אֲבָקָה.

NOUNS DENOTING DUST.

chant' (אִבְקַת רוֹכֵל)? There can scarcely be a doubt that the reference here is to extremely fine aromatic powders, composed of particles so light as to be easily blown away, and readily exhaling those sweet odours which give them distinctive character. Such powder is both visible and palpable,—thus differing from שַׁחַק. It is, moreover, soft as velvet to the touch, and very light; in these respects especially it differs, on the other hand, from עָפָר, which, as we shall show, means coarse and heavy dust.

These features of אֲבָקָה are observable also in אָבָק, which, however, is applied to dust of earth, so fine and light as to be lifted easily and blown about by wind, or stirred to form a cloud,—only too visible and disagreeable. Thus, Ezekiel (26 : 10), addressing Tyre on her impending destruction by Nebuchadnezzar, adopts peculiar phraseology to represent the conquering hosts as absolutely overpowering: 'Because of the overwhelming multitude of his horses, their dust (אֲבָקָם *i. e.* the fine dust raised by their hoofs) shall cover thee;' and Nahum (1 : 3) poetically pictures the divine dominion in the skies by saying, 'Cloud is the dust of his feet' (עָנָן אֲבַק רַגְלָיו). Isaiah in one passage (5 : 24) sets forth the close of the career of ungodly Israelites as one which others would not like even to behold; 'Their root shall be as putridity, and their blossom shall go up like fine dust' (כָּאָבָק), causing only annoyance to those around; while in another passage (29 : 5) he thus represents Jehovah's judgments as resistless, 'The multitude of thy strangers shall be like fine dust (כְּאָבָק דַּק), and the multitude of those dreadful in might like chaff passing away.' We have likewise already seen [1] that the furnace-soot cast by Moses and Aaron into the air was fitly designated 'fine dust' (אָבָק), Exod. 9 : 9. All these passages clearly prove that אָבָק applies to dust that is both fine and light, yet visible.

c. Of all the terms applied to dust, עָפָר occurs most frequently, and always in the sense of *coarse and heavy dust*. It thus differs from אָבָק and שַׁחַק in degree; the mass of the particles composing it is greater than in either of these instances. עָפָר assuredly is visible, and so distinctly palpable as to feel rough when touched.

The relation subsisting between עָפָר and אֲדָמָה [2] is noteworthy and

---

[1] Consider the remarks made at page 135.
[2] See the discussion on words signifying 'earth.'

significant; the former is the chief constituent of the latter. Accordingly, we read in Gen. 2:7 that God formed man, 'dust from the ground' (עָפָר מִן־הָאֲדָמָה); and in the sentence passed on him after the Fall, it was declared (Gen. 3:19), 'Dust (עָפָר) thou art, and unto dust (אֶל־עָפָר) shalt thou return,'—a truth repeated in the words of other writers, as in Eccl. 3:20, 'All are from the dust (מִן־הֶעָפָר), and all return to the dust' (אֶל־הֶעָפָר); Job 34:15, 'Man shall return to dust' (עָפָר); see moreover 10:9; 21:26; Psalm 103:14; 104:29.

So close, indeed, is the relation subsisting between עָפָר and אֲדָמָה that they are often interchanged, as practically identical. Thus, on the one hand, we read that Joshua and the elders of Israel (Josh. 7:6) and Job's three friends (Job 2:12) cast dust (עָפָר) upon their heads in token of mourning (see also Lam. 2:10; Ezekiel 27:30); and on the other hand that the Benjamite messenger, bearing the fatal tidings to Eli, came with his clothes rent and earth (אֲדָמָה) on his head (1 Sam. 4:12); while, after the completion of the Second Temple, the Israelites 'assembled, with fasting and with sackcloth, and earth (אֲדָמָה) upon them' (Nehem. 9:1). In the more poetic books especially, עָפָר is often employed as essentially identical with אֲדָמָה, and hence may safely be rendered, as in our English Versions, 'ground.' Thus Isaiah (2:19), depicting divine judgments on sinners, says that these 'shall go......into rock-caves and holes in the ground (מְחִלּוֹת עָפָר), from fear of the Lord;' Job (14:8) illustrates one of his arguments by referring to a tree whose 'trunk dies in the ground' (בֶּעָפָר), speaks (28:2) of iron as 'taken out of the ground' (מֵעָפָר), and of certain miserable human beings driven (30:6) to inhabit 'holes in the ground' (חֹרֵי עָפָר); see also 19:25. Specially noteworthy, in this connection, is the expression אַדְמַת עָפָר, in Dan. 12:2. Sometimes, however, we find the combination עֲפַר הָאָרֶץ, as in Gen. 13:16; 28:14; Ex. 8:12, 13; 2 Chron. 1:9; Isa. 40:12, etc. The idea of heaviness, associated with עָפָר, is further exhibited in its application to the rubbish or old plaster scraped off the walls of a house (Levit. 14:41, 42, 45), and the rubbish or dust of ruins (Neh. 3:34).

We can now appreciate the force of the terms employed in Deut. 28:24, describing one form of divine judgment upon Israel in apo-

NOUNS DENOTING DUST.   139

stasy, 'Jehovah shall make the rain of thy land (מְטַר אַרְצֶךָ) powder and heavy dust (אָבָק וְעָפָר); from heaven shall it descend upon thee until thou be consumed.'

Again, we may with perfect confidence decide on the correct reading of the Hebrew text in various passages. The probability, previously indicated,[1] that in Num. 19 : 17 we should read אֵפֶר instead of עָפָר, must now be felt to have become a certainty. Similarly, in 2 Kings 23 : 4, we must conclude that עֲפָרָם ('the dust of them') is rather to be read אֶפְרָם ('the ashes of them'). There we find it recorded that Josiah caused the Temple-officers to 'bring out from the Temple of Jehovah all the instruments (הַכֵּלִים) that had been made for Baal and for Astarte, and for all the host of heaven, and they burned them (וַיִּשְׂרְפֵם) outside Jerusalem......and carried away the ashes of them' (אֶפְרָם, not עֲפָרָם). The articles burned were wooden implements (כְּלִי עֵץ); as we now know, the residue of these, when fire has finished its transforming work, is designated אֵפֶר, not עָפָר. Similarly, in v. 6, when we read that the image of Astarte—which, as we learn otherwise, was made of wood—was brought out of the house of the Lord and burned, we must certainly conclude that the residue, which was afterwards beaten small, and then scattered upon graves of the common people, should be called אֵפֶר, not עָפָר,[2] *i. e.* 'ashes,' not 'coarse dust' (A.V. and R.V. 'powder').

Conversely, we must conclude that certain passages, incorrectly, have אֵפֶר instead of עָפָר, seeing that the whole context leads us to think of 'dust,' but not 'ashes.' Thus, in Mal. 3 : 21 [4 : 3 in English], it sounds somewhat strange to read, in the words addressed to those who fear the Lord, the assurance that the wicked 'shall be ashes (אֵפֶר) under the soles of your feet;' the correct reading must surely be 'dust' (עָפָר).[3] Again, Jeremiah, in one of his utterances against Israel (6 : 26), thus summons them to mourning and humiliation, 'Gird on sackcloth, and wallow in the ashes,' the Massoretic text in the latter clause being הִתְפַּלְּשִׁי בָאֵפֶר; but ashes are by no

---

[1] See the foot-note on page 131.

[2] On the other hand, in verses 12, 15, where we read that idolatrous altars were broken down (or smashed), עָפָר is properly employed to mark the form to which the materials had been reduced.

[3] In this and the other passages cited, σποδός is the rendering given by the Septuagint translators. The erroneous readings introduced by Hebrew copyists are thus of high antiquity.

means so plentiful as dust, and we must therefore rather read בְּעָפָר, 'in the dust,' especially when we consider the normative passage, Micah 1 : 10.¹ Finally, we may somewhat confidently correct the Massoretic text in Ezek. 27 : 30, which, remarkably, presents a twofold interchange of terms; describing the lamentation over the desolation of Tyre, by the mariners who used to frequent the merchant city, the prophet says, 'they shall cast up ashes (יַעֲלוּ אֵפֶר) on their heads, in the dust shall they wallow' (בְּעָפָר יִתְפַּלָּשׁוּ). Such an application of the terms is certainly more probable than that which is indicated in the received Hebrew text,—dust on the head, and ashes in which the wailers wallowed.

---

¹ The correct reading has been preserved here through the adjacence of the proper name בֵּית לְעַפְרָה, to which there is unmistakable reference in the following words, '[in the] dust do thou wallow' (עָפָר הִתְפַּלָּשִׁי).

ENGLISH INDEX.

Aged	58	Oil		47
Ancient	58	Old		53
Ashes	131	Parapet		12
Boundary-wall	9	Poor		81
Cliff	113	Pour out		92
Coal	40	Powder		136
Conceal, cover	66	Rain		105
Crag	113	Reserve		69
Dust	136	Rock		112
Exhausted	62	Rod		117
Flee	1	Sceptre		125
Flood	44	Sleep, slumber		26
Folly, fool	29	Staff, stick		117
Hide	66	Wash		15
Lion	22	Weary, weariness		63

HEBREW INDEX.

81	אביון	66	טמן	117	מקל	68	צפן		
136	אבק אבקה	62	יגע יגיע	118	משענת	58	קדמני		
138	אדמה	109	יורה	33	נבל נבלה	10	קיר		
31	אויל אולת	63	יעף	92	נבע	89	רָאשׁ		
131	אפר	47	יצהר	6	נדר	110	רביבים		
23	ארי אריה	97	יצק	27	נוּם	89	רוּשׁ		
56	בָּחוּר	58	ישיש	1	נוּם	15	רחץ		
54	בלה	26	יָשֵׁן	94	נסך	42	רצף רצפה		
3	ברח	53	יָשָׁן	35	נספל	89	רָשׁ		
9	גדר גדרה	17	כבס	55	נער	125	שבט		
22	גוּר	29	כסיל כסלוּת	28	נרדם	13	שׁגוּר		
40	גחלת	112	כפים	92	נתך	24	שחל		
106	גשם	23	כפיר	111	סנריר	136	שחק		
83	דל דלה	123	כתף	35	סכל סכלוּת	44, 19	שטף		
85	דש	60	לאה	113	סלע	123	שכם		
133	דֶשֶׁן	24	לביא	71	סתר	49	שמן		
16	הדיח	24	ליש	63	עיף עיפה	116	שן		
55	זקן זקנה	44	מבוּל	74	עלם	26	שֵׁנָה		
111	זרזיף	109	מורה	81	עני	110	שעיר		
108	זרם	120	מטה	137	עפר	100	שפך		
77	חבא חבה	105	מטר	62	פגר	57	שׂיבה		
85	חבט	95	מפכה	42	פחם	61	תלאה		
8	חומה	88	מספן	135	פיח	27	תנוּמה		
13	חיץ	12	מעקה	95	פסל	28	תרדמה		

www.ingramcontent.com/pod-product-compliance
Lightning Source LLC
Chambersburg PA
CBHW070911160426
43193CB00011B/1427